WHAT'S UP IN HEAVEN?

What The Bible Teaches
About Immediate and Eternal
Heaven

Dr. Neale B. Oliver

What's Up in Heaven?
What The Bible Teaches About Immediate and Eternal Heaven
2022© by Dr. Neale B. Oliver
All rights reserved. Published 2022.

BIBLE SCRIPTURES

Unless otherwise noted, all Scripture quotations are taken from the Holman Christian Standard Bible (HCSB), Copyright 1999, 2000, 2002, 2003, 2009 by Holman Publishers. Used by permission. HCSB is a federally registered trademark of Holman Bible Publishers.

Scripture quotations marked (TLB) are taken from The Living Bible, copyright 1971. Used by permission of Tyndale House Publisher, Inc. Carol Stream, Illinois 60188. All rights reserved.

Scripture quotations marked (MSG) are taken from The Message. Copyright 1993, 1994, 1995, 1996, 2000, 2001, 2002 by Eugene H. Peterson. Used by permission of NavPress. All rights reserved. Represented by Tyndale House Publishers, Inc.

Scriptures marked (KJV) are taken from the KING JAMES VERSION (KJV): KING JAMES VERSION, public domain.

Printed in the United States of America
Spirit Media
www.spiritmedia.us

Spirit Media, and our logos are trademarks of Spirit Media

1249 Kildaire Farm Rd STE 112
Cary, NC 27511
(919) 629-9899

Religion & Spirituality | Christian Books & Bibles | Spiritual Growth
Paperback ISBN: 978-1-958304-00-6
Hardback ISBN: 978-1-958304-01-3
Audiobook ISBN: 978-1-958304-02-0
eBook ISBN: 978-1-958304-03-7
Library of Congress Control Number: 2022908442

SPIRIT MEDIA

Register This New Book

Benefits of Registering*

- FREE replacements of lost or damaged books
- FREE audiobook—Get to the Point by Kevin White
- FREE information about new titles and other freebies

www.spiritmedia.us/register
*See our website for requirements and limitations

ENDORSEMENTS

With the fear of the unknown fueling anxiety in our culture, Dr. Oliver does a masterful job, carefully unpacking two of life's major mysteries. Those being: What exactly is up in Heaven? And how do we get there?

Backed and saturated with Scripture, this book will equip and encourage every reader to overcome those fears and to put more confidence in the God of the Universe. Our world needs to see more than ever the beautiful picture of what God has prepared for those who love Him! This book is a peace-giver, confidence-builder, and an anxiety-killer. I strongly recommend it to young and old!

—Jake McEntire
Creator, Writer & Producer of the motion picture Run The Race; Director of Development for Rising Light Ridge with the Tim Tebow Foundation

Dr. Oliver knocked it out of the park with *All About The Second Coming of Christ* and once again with his new book, *What's Up In Heaven?* If you have questions about Heaven and want them answered with biblically sound theology and backed with Scriptures straight out of God's own Word, then this is the book for you! Dr. Oliver has such a way of bringing Heaven to life that it makes it sound sweeter every day. Grab one for yourself and a friend, or better yet, have your friends and family get one, and start a Bible study together. This book will challenge you to see how much the Lord loves us and what we have in store for the future.

—Teresa Graff
Worship Leader/Vocalist, Shepherd's Valley Cowboy Church, Alvarado, Texas; Worship Leader, Cleburne Christian Business Club, Ambassador & Director on the board of The Cleburne Chamber of Commerce; Owner/Stylist, The Strand Hair Studio, Tanning & Boutique, Cleburne, Texas

After reading Dr. Oliver's *What's Up In Heaven?* I used it to preach a six-week sermon series on Heaven. This is one of the easiest to understand and most relatable books I've ever come across dealing with death, eternity, and what takes place afterwards. As a pastor of over forty years, I highly recommend this book.

—*Rev. Jacky Newton*
Pastor of Franklinton Baptist Church, Pleasureville, Kentucky

Being a youth pastor, I read *What's Up In Heaven?* from a student's perspective. I even studied the first two chapters with my student discipleship group. This book is very clear and concise in delivering the message of Heaven. I love how Scripture intertwines with the point Dr. Oliver is conveying. I would highly recommend this book to anyone and everyone!

—*Eric Waits*
Youth Pastor, First Baptist Grandview, Texas

What's Up In Heaven? is another home-run for you. It will bring joy and peace to those who are anxiously waiting for the Savior to come. This is a must-read for every Christian. It will bring hope and assurance to all who have placed their faith in Jesus. Congratulations on another outstanding book.

—*Dave Childers*
Retired Associate Professor of Communications, Palm Beach State College, Lake Worth, Florida

To my children, Roger, Ryne, and Robbi-Ann,
who have made life on Earth a slice of Heaven.

TABLE OF CONTENTS

ACKNOWLEDGEMENT

No book is ever an individual effort. Many people made this book possible.

First, to my beautiful wife, Glynis. You are a blessing and a gift from God. From our marriage on Earth to our eternal life in Heaven, "You are my forever always."

To my parents, Roger and Lil Oliver, who passed away during the writing of this book. I know you are with Jesus, walking in His presence. Writing this book has been therapeutic for me. I look forward to the day I enter Heaven, and to see your shining faces again, forever.

To the people of Henderson Street Baptist Church in Cleburne, Texas. As we continue to partner together in the Lord's work, I am blessed to be your pastor. You are encouraging and uplifting. It's a joy to work with you. I am blessed by God to have you in my life.

To my editing team, Carolyn, Debbie, Donna, Eloise, John, Kathleen, Ray, Roger, Steve, and Tammy. Your help with the manuscript was invaluable. Your feedback helped me believe this book was worthy of being published.

To my friend Steve Waits. We have been through thick and thin together. You have been there for me when I needed a friend. You have always supported me and been honest with me. For that, I am thankful. May God continue to bless you and your family.

To Paul and Linda Wicker. One of my greatest victories in ministry is to have led you to the Lord and baptized you. From a near-death experience without Jesus to eternal life with Jesus. Your last breath on Earth was your first breath in Heaven.

To the men's prayer ministry at Henderson Street Baptist Church. Many will inherit the Kingdom of Heaven because of your faithful prayers. I look forward to our early Monday morning prayer time together. Let's eat some bacon!

To every pastor and minister who gets their hands on this book. You may not agree with everything in this book. That's OK! I encourage you to write your book. I believe every pastor can and should write a book. Find your passion and put it on paper. It will bless you and it will bless those who read your words.

PREFACE: ABOUT THIS BOOK

Would it surprise you to know that many Christians spend more time researching their vacation destination than they do their eternal destination? We know more about Hawaii than we do Heaven. If you're a Christian, Heaven is not a vacation destination. It's your eternal home, the place where you will live FOREVER! It's Jesus' hometown, and He is there preparing your home right now (John 14:1-3).

What's Up In Heaven? comes from over 35 years of study, research, and teaching about our spiritual home. This book gives you a view of Heaven from the moment you die to the moment you step into the New Heaven and the New Earth.

What's Up In Heaven? is formatted with questions and answers, because it's the best way we learn. As a young child, how many times did you ask, "Why?" and someone gave you the answer?

Included at the end of each chapter is a seven-point review, along with five big questions. There is a group discussion guide for large groups, small groups, or a one-on-one setting.

There are many books on Heaven. I do not intend to repeat what other authors have written, but to help you discover what the Bible teaches about Heaven.

INTRODUCTION

Have you been excited about an upcoming event and you couldn't wait for the day to arrive? The closer it got, the more excited you got? Christmas is one of those events. I didn't sleep the night of Christmas Eve, and I was up at the crack of dawn.

Christmas Day was great, but it pales compared to the day I got my first pair of Converse All Stars. I was eight years old when dad decided I could have a pair of Chuck Taylor's All Stars. Every day, I went to mom and asked, "How many more days?" She told me five more days or four more days. I know mom and dad were waiting for payday, but I did not understand that at the time. I only wanted to put those new white Converse All Stars on my feet.

I don't know whether I wore them down, or they could see how excited I was and just gave in, but two days before payday, mom took me to the local department store and bought me the best gift I had ever received. I'm not sure what shoes I wore into the store, but I know what shoes I wore when I flew out of the store. I was so excited; I jumped and landed on both feet, spun around three times, like a dog chasing its tail, and took off across the parking lot to the station wagon. That's right, we had a station wagon! In those new shoes, I ran faster, jumped higher, and climbed quicker. I challenged every boy to a race and beat them going away. I took care of those shoes, cleaning them each night with a wet washcloth, and setting them on the floor right beside the bed. They were the last thing I took off my feet at night, and the first thing I put on my feet the next morning.

Why do I tell you that story? Because Heaven is the best gift you will ever receive, and I'm excited to tell you about it. Jesus is building our eternal hometown right now. It's beyond our imaginations. We cannot fathom in our limited minds the beauty and majesty of Heaven. While God doesn't give us complete information about Heaven, which I believe is for obvious reasons, He gives us enough to whet our appetites, and get us excited about living with Him for eternity in His home.

The idea for, *What's Up In Heaven?* came from a lady in the church I pastor. As I closed the teaching series on All About The Second Coming of Christ, I asked, "What's one thing you learned?" She said, "I learned there are two Heavens. I thought there was just one!"

Many Christians believe in just one Heaven, but there are two. Immediate Heaven, the place you go to when you die, and Eternal Heaven, the place you will live forever. It's a fact! In Revelation 21:3 (KJV), John said, "I saw a new heaven and new earth, for the first heaven and the first earth had passed away." What John saw was Eternal Heaven from the viewpoint of Immediate Heaven. How?

Revelation 4:1, "After this I looked, and there in heaven was an open door. The first voice that I had heard speaking to me like a trumpet said, 'Come up here, and I will show you what must take place after this.'"

Now, I want you to understand what is happening here. John was "caught up" to Heaven so he could record what takes place from Immediate Heaven to Eternal Heaven. In the Book of Revelation, John has four visions. Many theologians divide the visions this way:

1. Vision One: The Kingdom from Jesus' Perspective (Revelation 1-3)

2. Vision Two: The Kingdom from a Heavenly Perspective (Revelation 4-16)

3. Vision Three: The Kingdom from an Earthly Perspective (Revelation 17-21:8)

4. Vision Four: The Kingdom from an Eternal Perspective (Revelation 21:9-22:7)

These visions are of first Heaven and last Heaven, as well as present Earth and the New Earth. John's vision starts with Christ's Ascension after his Resurrection and ends with your entrance into the New Jerusalem. This is important because we live in the period called, "The Last Hour," or "The Last Days," or "The End Times."

As I did in my first book, *All About The Second Coming of Christ*, I have taken the liberty to capitalize Earth, Heaven, Hell, and the Lake of Fire, as I believe they are actual places. I have capitalized Satan, Devil, and anti-Christ, for I believe they are actual people. I have capitalized the

River of Living Water and the Tree of Life, for they are significant to the New Jerusalem and deserve the proper noun form. I have capitalized the words "Resurrection" and "Ascension" when they relate to Jesus' physical Resurrection and Ascension. These are two important doctrines and events in the Bible.

So, are you ready to learn what the Bible teaches about Heaven? I hope and pray that what you read will encourage and inspire you, as you learn about your heavenly home.

So, let's look at *What's Up in Heaven?*

Until He Comes,

Dr. Neale B. Oliver

PART ONE: IMMEDIATE HEAVEN

(THE PLACE YOU GO WHEN YOU DIE)

CHAPTER ONE:
THE FIRST HEAVEN

My first experience with death was as a young eleven-year-old boy. Friends of my mom and dad lost their only son in a car accident. Ricky's death hit me hard. I grew up in a family with three older sisters. While there were many boys in our neighborhood in the 1970's, Ricky was one I respected. So, when he died, it was like I lost my big brother. At that point, death became a reality for me. Ricky's family are Christians, so I believe he is in Heaven, and has been there since 1973.

Long before I knew I would pastor and console families who have lost a loved one, Ricky's death made me realize there's a place called Heaven, and it's the place believers go when they die.

Death is a certainty for human beings on the Earth. We are born, we live, and then we die. The only one who can interrupt this natural process is Jesus. There is a day coming when He will descend from Heaven and rapture Christians from the Earth. We will meet Him in the sky, and He will usher us back to Heaven (1 Thessalonians 4:13-18). If you have a believing loved one who died, you can take comfort in the fact, as they took their last breath on Earth, they took their first breath in Heaven. Death is transitioning from Earth to Heaven.

WHY DOES HEAVEN EXIST IN THE FIRST PLACE?

Let's answer this question from two perspectives. First, in relation to time, Heaven is very close. Death is imminent for all of us. When we wake up in the morning, we have no guarantee we will make it to our pillow at night. Today may be our last day on this Earth. With this in mind, Heaven is very close.

> 2 Corinthians 5:8, "And we are confident and satisfied to be out of the body and at home with the Lord."

> Philippians 1:21, "For me, living is Christ and dying is gain."

Second, in relation to proximity, Heaven is very close. Could our entrance into Heaven when we die be just a dimension or doorway? Before you dismiss this, look at the following passages in the Bible.

When the Apostle John was taken up to Heaven, he says he saw an open door:

> Revelation 4:1, "After this I looked, and there in heaven was an open door."

This is similar to the prophet Ezekiel's vision:

> Ezekiel 1:1, "In the thirtieth year, in the fourth month, on the fifth day of the month, while I was among the exiles by the Chebar Canal, the heavens opened and I saw visions of God."

In the New Testament, Heaven opened as a door to Jesus' baptism:

> Matthew 3:16, "After Jesus was baptized, He went up immediately from the water. The heavens suddenly opened for Him, and He saw the Spirit of God descending like a dove and coming down on Him."

Stephen saw Heaven opened:

> Acts 7:55-56, "But Stephen, filled by the Holy Spirit, gazed into heaven. He saw God's glory, with Jesus standing at the right hand of God, and he said, 'Look! I see the heavens opened and the Son of Man standing at the right hand of God!'"

Peter saw Heaven opened:

> Acts 10:11, "He saw heaven opened and an object that resembled a large sheet coming down, being lowered by its four corners to the earth."

The Apostle John has two other visions where he sees into Heaven:

> Revelation 11:19, "God's sanctuary in heaven was opened, and the ark of His covenant appeared in His sanctuary. There were flashes of lightning, rumblings of thunder, an earthquake, and severe hail."

> Revelation 15:5, "After this I looked, and the heavenly sanctuary—the tabernacle of testimony—was opened."

Heaven opened when John saw the Faithful and True Rider on the white horse coming to the Earth:

> Revelation 19:11, "Then I saw heaven opened, and there was a white horse. Its rider is called Faithful and True, and He judges and makes war in righteousness."

Could it be possible that when Jesus ascended to Heaven in Acts 1:9, after He disappeared from the apostles, He passed from Earth to Heaven through an open door? I'll leave that for you to ponder.

WHAT WILL WE NOT DO IN HEAVEN?

I've read many books on Heaven and they always ask, "What will we do in Heaven?" It's a good question, even a necessary question. But let's flip the coin, and answer the question nobody asks, "What will we not do in Heaven?" Knowing what we will not do is just as important as knowing what we will do.

In Heaven we will not be bored. Those who know nothing of Heaven want you to believe that it's boring and all you will do is sit on a cloud, wearing a white robe, flapping your wings, and playing a harp. None of those things are true.

Heaven will not be boring because God is not boring. Imagine Moses at the burning bush. The children of Israel crossing the Red Sea. Shadrach, Meshach, and Abed-nego in the fiery furnace. Daniel in the lion's den. Peter walking on the water. Israel fleeing Jerusalem during the Tribulation Period. Jesus returning with His armies at the Second Coming. When you imagine those events from the Bible, is there anything boring about them? No! Your imagination is never boring, and neither is the Bible. I agree with Robert Jeffress, pastor of First Baptist Church of Dallas, when he says, "But there is nothing boring about God. He is exceeding and eternally fascinating: just look at the present world He has created for us to live in." And I would add, "The future world He is creating for us right now."

The Earth created by God is exciting and exhilarating. It's not boring. We have mountains to climb, sunsets to see, beaches to walk, rivers to fish, and lakes to ski. There are cruise ships to take us to exotic destinations, and airplanes to fly us to the great wonders in the world. God has created everything for our entertainment. There is nothing boring in the world. We get bored because we live in an imperfect body that tires of the mundane and routine things of life. But in Heaven, we have a perfect body, and there's nothing mundane or routine in Heaven.

In Heaven today, there is great excitement, anticipating Jesus' Rapture of the church. This could happen at any moment, and I promise you, it will not be boring.

Second, in Heaven we will not sin. That alone will make Heaven great. Let's look at two passages from the Bible where Paul states that sin and the unsaved sinner will not be in Heaven:

> Galatians 5:19-21, "Now the works of the flesh are obvious: sexual immorality, moral impurity, promiscuity, idolatry, sorcery, hatreds, strife, jealousy, outbursts of anger, selfish ambitions, dissensions, factions, envy, drunkenness, carousing,

and anything similar. I tell you about these things in advance—as I told you before—that those who practice such things will not inherit the kingdom of God."

1 Corinthians 6:9-10, "Do you not know that the unjust will not inherit God's kingdom? Do not be deceived: No sexually immoral people, idolaters, adulterers, or anyone practicing homosexuality, no thieves, greedy people, drunkards, verbally abusive people, or swindlers will inherit God's kingdom."

Paul points out that those who practice these sins will not inherit the Kingdom of God. But notice what Jesus says about those who are cursed by sin:

Matthew 25:41,46, "Then He will also say to those on the left, 'Depart from Me, you who are cursed, into the eternal fire prepared for the Devil and his angels!' (demons)... And they will go away into eternal punishment, but the righteous into eternal life."

The Bible is crystal clear, there will be no sin in Heaven.

WHAT WILL WE DO IN HEAVEN?

Since we are not bored, and we will not sin, what will we do in Heaven? We will worship and we will work. On Earth, we worship who we know, but who we do not see. In Heaven, we will worship who we know and who we see. I believe worship will be our primary activity in Heaven, but it will not be our only activity in Heaven.

I believe we will also work. "But, Neale, I've worked my entire life on Earth. I just want to rest when I get to Heaven!" I understand. I've known people who complain their job is exhausting, but their salary is so good, they can't afford to quit. That is not the case in Heaven. Work in Heaven is never exhausting. I know because Heaven is never exhausting. Heaven is exciting, breathtaking, and exhilarating. It's perfection! You may not like your job on Earth, but you are going to love your job in Heaven, because it will be a job that fits your gifts and talents. It's a job given to you by the One who knows you best—God. When you get to Heaven, you will want to work. You will be so excited, you just can't sit still.

Think of it this way. Have you ever been to a place that was exhilarating and energetic? You were excited and wanted to be a part of the event, so you talked to the person in charge and said, "What can I do to help?" That's how you feel when you get to Heaven—excited and energetic. You're going to want to pitch in and help. Remember, you're not in an imperfect body in Heaven. You have a new and perfect body. And with it, you will worship and work. Two things you have always done, and will always do, even in Heaven.

WILL YOU BE MARRIED TO YOUR SPOUSE IN HEAVEN?

No! In Matthew 22:23-28, Jesus was confronted by the Sadducees, who shared a story of a woman who married seven brothers. They all died, leaving her with no children. The woman dies, and the Sadducees want to know whose wife she'd be in Heaven.

With this question, the Sadducees' attempt to trap Jesus, but He turns the table on them and exposes their lack of knowledge of the Scriptures:

> Matthew 22:29-30, "Jesus answered them, 'You are deceived, because you don't know the Scriptures or the power of God.' For in the resurrection they neither marry nor are given in marriage but are like angels in heaven."

Jesus says in Heaven, there will be no marriage. This does not mean a husband and wife do not have a relationship in Heaven. I believe they will. I struggle to believe Glynis and I will spend most of our life together on Earth, but not be together in Heaven. There are godly couples that are married fifty, sixty, even seventy-five years on Earth, so it's only natural to believe that they will be together in Heaven. Married? No! Together? Yes!

Why is there no marriage in Heaven? First, there's no need for marriage in Heaven. When God created marriage on Earth, it was for a particular need. Adam needed a companion, so God created Eve (Genesis 2:18-24). Eve was God's solution to give Adam a "helper" for life. In Heaven, we do not need a "helper." We will be with God, who meets all of our needs.

Second, there's no marriage because reproduction does not exist in Heaven. A reason for marriage on Earth was to fill the Earth with humanity. Heaven is full of believers who inhabit Heaven because of their faith in Jesus Christ.

Third, there's no marriage in Heaven because we are symbolically married to Christ. Marriage on Earth is a picture of our marriage to Jesus in Heaven. Marriage is a relationship of a bride (woman) and groom (man), who become one flesh (Genesis 2:24; Matthew 19:5; Ephesians 5:31).

In Ephesians 5:22-33, the Apostle Paul describes the "husband and wife" relationship. In this passage, Paul writes about the marital roles of the husband and wife. I use this passage as part of my pre-marital counseling, and I read this passage during the wedding ceremony.

Is it about the earthly husband and wife relationship? Yes, I believe it is. Yet, in verse 32, Paul clearly states that he is talking about the relationship between Christ and the church. This is one of those passages in the Bible that has a double-reference. It emphasizes both the earthly horizontal relationship we have as husband and wife, and the Heavenly vertical relationship we have with Jesus. One must remember, the most important relationship in Heaven is with Jesus. He's the whole reason we are in Heaven.

My parents, Roger and Lillian Oliver, were married sixty-one years, eight months, and six days on this Earth. That comes to 22,531 days, including Leap Year. Of those days, there were very few they spent apart. The exceptions were mom's annual visits to Frances Conley, her sister who lived in Oak Ridge, Tennessee, and dad's annual trips to Kentucky Lake with his nephew, Charles Marcum, and a long-time friend, Donald Burchett. Aside from that, they spent every day together.

Mom died on December 23, 2020, and dad died ten days later, on January 2, 2021. If they could have died together, I believe they would have. Here's what I know. They stepped into Heaven, mom first and dad right behind her. After being separated for ten days on Earth, they arrived in Heaven a few seconds apart.

Over the last ten years, dad and I had many conversations about dying, and he always said, "I pray every day that God takes me first." He knew mom could survive without him, but he could not survive without her.

Dad depended on mom for everything, and when she died, he didn't know what to do.

After mom died, I left the hospital and drove to their house. I told dad that mom passed away, and the first thing he said, "You know, I prayed every day that God would take me first. That didn't happen, and it's OK! Now, I pray God takes me as soon as possible." God answered his prayer ten days later.

When people ask me what happened, I tell them, "It's a tragic story, but it's a great love story. Mom died of a stroke, and dad died of a broken heart." He didn't want to live on Earth without his precious wife and best friend. After 10 days of separation, Jesus came for my dad, and now he and mom are "Together Forever." That's become a motto for our family when we talk about mom and dad. They are together forever in Heaven.

I know with absolute certainty that Roger and Lillian Oliver are walking the streets of Heaven together. I rejoice knowing they are with Jesus. They are experiencing the riches and glory of Heaven, and they're reunited with their believing family and friends. My heart leaps with joy knowing they are living out their glorious reward, and will do so for eternity. Death has not taken their life, it has renewed, restored, and revived their life. As much as they lived on Earth, it can't even compare to the life they are living in Heaven.

The truth is, we're going to die. Death is part of life. I miss my mom and dad, our Monday conversations, and being able to pick up the phone and hear their voices. But I am comforted knowing I will see them again and it will be forever.

To mom and dad: You lived life on this Earth together, and now you are living eternal life in Heaven together. From Debbie, Leatha, Laura, and myself, we wouldn't want it any other way.

I pray you have the same assurance my parents have. If you don't, then I encourage you to believe and receive the One who turns death into life. His name is Jesus Christ, and He died on the Cross so you can live with Him in a perfect paradise called Heaven. And like Roger and Lillian Oliver, you can be "Together Forever" with Jesus.

7 Points of Review

1. There are two Heavens. Immediate Heaven is the place you go to when you die. Eternal Heaven is the New Earth and New Jerusalem, the place you will live forever.

2. Heaven exists as a reward for believers. God wants to lavish on you His very best.

3. Heaven is big. It comes from the Hebrew word "shameh" or "shamayim," which refers to sky and outer space. Heaven, God's home, is infinite. The universe is big, but Heaven is even bigger.

4. Heaven is close, because you could die at any moment. But it's also close because it could be a dimension or a doorway. Ezekiel, John, Stephen, Peter speak of seeing Heaven open, like a door.

5. In Heaven, you are not bored, and you will not sin. In Heaven, you will worship with Jesus. On Earth, we worship Him, but we don't see Him. In Heaven, we will worship Him and we will see Him.

6. In Heaven, you will work. God is a worker, and He created you to work. Adam and Eve worked in the Garden of Eden before the Fall, and they worked on the Earth after the Fall. The work you do in Heaven is exciting and exhilarating, and it fits your gifts and talents.

7. You are not married in Heaven, because there's no need for marriage in Heaven. The most important relationship you have in Heaven is not earthly, but heavenly with Jesus.

1. Who are the two groups of people who do not believe in Heaven? What do they believe about life and death on Earth?

    _____

    _____

    _____

    _____

2. What do the Hebrew words "shameh" or "shamayim" and the Greek word "ouranos" say about Heaven?

    _____

    _____

    _____

    _____

3. It is possible that the entrance into Heaven could be a doorway? Explain:

    _____

    _____

    _____

    _____

4. Why do people believe Heaven is boring? Why will Heaven not be boring?

_____

_____

_____

_____

5. What are the three reasons there's no marriage in Heaven?

_____

_____

_____

_____

Group Discussion Guide

MOTIVATION:

• Many people look at dying as the end of life, but Heaven is the beginning of life.

• Use a concordance, and read the verses that mention "eternal life." As a group, discuss how Heaven is the beginning of eternal life.

EXAMINATION:

• Discuss how Heaven is not boring because God is not boring. Use the following events from the Bible as talking-points:

    1. Noah's Ark–Genesis 7

    2. David and Goliath–1 Samuel 17

    3. The Fiery Furnace–Daniel 3

    4. Jonah and the Whale–Jonah 1-4

    5. The Feeding of the 5,000–Matthew 14

    6. The Transfiguration–Matthew 17

    7. The Raising of Lazarus–John 11

    Many of the events recorded in the Bible are miraculous and not boring. If God is not boring, and what He does is not boring, then we can conclude Heaven is not boring.

- You are not bored in Heaven, because you will work in Heaven. On Earth, many people complain work is boring. Read: Colossians 3:23-24. Discuss how putting these two verses into practice can bring purpose to your work.

APPLICATION:

- One reason Heaven exists is to reward you. To God, Heaven is not enough of a reward for you. He wants to lavish His blessings on you. Truth: You don't have to wait until you get to Heaven for God to pour out His blessings on you. You can have them now. Read John 10:10; Matthew 6:33 and 7:7.

- One thing you will do in Heaven is worship God. What can you do to elevate your worship of God on Earth? As you attend church, look for ways to raise your level of worship.

CHAPTER TWO:
A REAL PLACE
CALLED HEAVEN

If you're like me, you were told as a child that carrots improve your vision, toads give you warts, cracking your knuckles gives you arthritis, swimming right after you eat will give you cramps, and it takes seven years to digest gum. But these old wives' tales are false. I know a friend who loves carrots, but his glasses are as thick as a coke bottle. I've been cracking my knuckles most of my life, and I don't have arthritis. Many things we are told are not true.

Take, for example, Heaven. Many people don't believe it's an actual place. They know Earth is real because they can see it, touch it, and experience it, but they do not believe Heaven is real. People think the same about God. They can't see Him, touch Him, or talk face-to-face with Him, so He cannot be real.

The Apostle Paul says the created world screams the existence of God, and no one has an excuse for not believing in Him.

> Romans 1:20, "For His invisible attributes, that is, His eternal power and divine nature, have been clearly seen since the creation of the world, being understood through what He has made. As a result, people are without excuse."

Look at the mountains and the oceans. Or lie underneath the stars on a clear night. God created each and they prove He exists. You and I touch God every day by living and walking on the Earth. Since God is real, and the world He created is real, doesn't it make sense that Heaven is real?

HOW CAN YOU KNOW WITH ABSOLUTE CERTAINTY HEAVEN IS REAL?

The word "Heaven" appears over 600 times in the Bible. Since Jesus came from Heaven and He knows all about Heaven, we should believe what He says.

Let's return once again to Matthew 22 and Jesus' conversation with the Sadducees. Let's not look at it from the perspective of marriage, but from the perspective of resurrection.

Matthew 22:23-33, "The same day some Sadducees, who say there is no resurrection, came up to Him and questioned Him: 'Teacher, Moses said, if a man dies, having no children, his brother is to marry his wife and raise up offspring for his brother. Now there were seven brothers among us. The first got married and died. Having no offspring, he left his wife to his brother. The same happened to the second also, and the third, and so to all seven. Then, last of all, the woman died. In the resurrection, therefore, whose wife will she be of the seven? For they all had married her.' Jesus answered them, 'You are deceived, because you don't know the Scriptures or the power of God. For in the resurrection they neither marry nor are given in marriage, but are like angels in heaven. Now concerning the resurrection of the dead, haven't you read what was spoken to you by God: I am the God of Abraham and the God of Isaac and the God of Jacob? He is not the God of the dead, but of the living.' And when the crowds heard this, they were astonished at His teaching."

In this passage, Jesus gives us three pieces of evidence from His own mouth that Heaven is real:

First, Jesus refutes the Sadducees' false belief in the resurrection of the dead. It's important that you understand who the Sadducees are:

- They were a priestly organization in Israel, along with the Pharisees.

- They revered Moses and accepted only the Pentateuch (Genesis–Deuteronomy).

- They believed humans ceased to exist at the moment of physical death.

- They did not believe in the resurrection of the dead.

- They were the elite of Jerusalem controlling the Sanhedrin and the High Priesthood.

- They were more politically minded than spiritually minded.

- They compromised with the pagan and secular leadership of Rome for control in Israel.

When they approached Jesus with this illustration, it's likely they had used it successfully when they debated the Pharisees, who believed in the resurrection of the dead. They did not realize Jesus was on a different level than the Pharisees, and it didn't take Him long to put them in their place. They were mistaken about the resurrection, and Jesus sets them straight. He believed in the resurrection of the dead, and was going to prove it with His own Resurrection in a couple of days.

Second, Jesus says Heaven is real because the resurrection is real. In verse 30, Jesus gives a new teaching. It's found nowhere else in the Bible. Jesus takes the Sadducees' illustration and shreds it. They didn't believe in the resurrection of the dead, but Jesus shows them, through the marriage illustration, that the dead must be resurrected to Heaven to enter the most important relationship in the universe, the heavenly marriage of Jesus to His bride. On a prophetical note, this marriage takes place in Heaven (Revelation 19:6-9).

Third, Jesus says He is the God of the living, not the dead. Since the Sadducees believed in only the Pentateuch, Jesus uses their Scripture to prove them wrong. In verse 32, Jesus is quoting Exodus 3:6, "I am the God of Abraham, Isaac, and Jacob." He uses the present tense, "I am," not the past tense, "I was." By doing this, Jesus was stating Abraham, Isaac, and Jacob are alive. Jesus will always be the God of the living.

You can know Heaven is real because Jesus was resurrected to Heaven, and His Resurrection guarantees your Resurrection.

> 1 Corinthians 15:20-23, "But now Christ has been raised from the dead, the firstfruits of those who have fallen asleep. For since death came through a man, the resurrection of the dead also comes through a man. For just as in Adam all die, so also in Christ, all will be made alive. But each in his own order: Christ, the firstfruits; afterward, at His coming, those who belong to Christ."

WHERE IS HEAVEN RIGHT NOW?

It's where God is. The Bible describes three heavens. The first Heaven is the sky, Earth's atmosphere, where the birds fly. The second Heaven is outer space, the solar system, the milky way, the galaxy. It's a vast space. Bigger than any of us can fathom. It's the stuff of science fiction. The third Heaven is the home of God. It's beyond the universe.

Where is Heaven right now? I'm not sure, but biblical research can help us find out. In Revelation 21:1-2, the Apostle John saw a New Heaven and a New Earth, with a New Jerusalem coming down from the third Heaven, the present home of God. Since it's "coming down out of heaven," we can conclude it's somewhere above the Earth beyond outer space.

When Jesus left the Earth at his Ascension (Acts 1:9-11), Luke said He ascended as the disciples watched. A cloud took Him away, out of their sight. In Revelation 4:1, John saw an open door, and a voice that told him to, "come up here." Where is "here?" It must be Heaven, where John sees what must take place.

These three examples refer to Heaven as "up" beyond the Earth. Now, I know what you are thinking. How can Heaven be up for a person in America and Australia, when they are pointing in different directions? There is one direction that is "up" regardless of where you are on the Earth. That direction is north. It is a fixed position, whether you are in America or Australia. Fix your eyes on the North Star and you will see the other stars rotate around it. I believe the Bible shows Heaven is North.

The psalmist believes that God is from the North.

> Psalm 75:6-7 (KJV), "For promotion cometh neither from the east, nor from the west, nor from the south. But God is the judge: he putteth down one, and setteth up another."

When Satan tried to ascend his throne above God's throne, it was to the North.

> Isaiah 14:13-14, "I will ascend to the heavens; I will set up my throne above the stars of God. I will sit on the mount of the gods' assembly, in the remotest parts of the North. I will ascend above the highest clouds; I will make myself like the Most High."

So, right now, Heaven is up beyond the clouds (first Heaven), and beyond outer space (second Heaven), to the home of God (third Heaven).

IS IMMEDIATE HEAVEN TEMPORARY AND ETERNAL AT THE SAME TIME?

Immediate Heaven is temporary, in the sense that it's not our final eternal home. But Jesus will change that when you step into Eternal Heaven. There will be nothing temporary about the New Heaven, New Earth, and New Jerusalem. They are the most permanent and forever place you will ever experience.

Immediate Heaven is temporary because it's not a Christian's final destination. It is a fantastic place, because God is there, but it's not our final, eternal home.

So, if Immediate Heaven is temporary, is it eternal? YES! Remember, the moment you're saved, you become eternal.

> John 3:16, "For God loved the world in this way: He gave His one and only Son, so that everyone who believes in Him will not perish but have eternal life."

> Romans 6:23, "For the wages of sin is death, but the gift of God is eternal life in Christ Jesus our Lord."

As Christians, you and I are eternal now and when we die, so it makes sense that the place we go to when we die is eternal, even though it's temporary.

WHAT WILL LIFE BE LIKE IN HEAVEN?

Joy will definitely be part of what we experience in Heaven, because we have entered God's presence for eternity. Joy is better than happiness, because happiness is based on circumstance. I am happy because I get good grades, because I graduated, or because I got a raise. Joy is regardless of circumstances. You have joy, even in tough times, because Jesus is your strength. I'm sad my mom and dad died. But I have joy knowing they are in Heaven.

God wants you to enjoy life. But He knows the things of the world that seem fun can hurt you. There are countless people who choose worldly things when they're in their twenties, yet by the time they reach their fifties, they are paying the price. I've seen pictures of young women addicted to meth, and fifteen years later, they are so skinny and strung out that you can't recognize them.

What sounds fun is often false and leads to ruin. God gives you great joy when you live life within the boundaries of the Bible. If you and I choose to follow the Bible, we will experience the abundant life (John 10:10).

Another characteristic of Immediate Heaven, you will enjoy the fellowship of other believers. We were part of a family, and that doesn't change in Heaven. We're reunited with our family and friends that have died, and we will have fellowship with those believing family members that we never knew on Earth. For example, my grandfather, Payton Oliver, died before I was born. I never knew him on Earth, but I will know him in Heaven. We can say the same for the great men and women of the Bible. Moses, Ruth, David, Esther, Isaiah, Daniel, Hosea, Malachi, Peter, John, Mary Magdalene, Paul, Timothy, the thief on the cross, and many, many more we will see and talk to in Heaven.

The last characteristic of Immediate Heaven you will enjoy is true rest. This is more than physical rest, it's spiritual rest. The sinful life on Earth can take its toll on you, your body, your mind, your soul, and your emotions. In Heaven, sin is nowhere to be found. Imagine taking a deep breath and exhaling all the weariness of sin. Jesus gives us a picture of this true rest when He says:

> Matthew 11:28, "Come to Me, all of you who are weary and burdened, and I will give you rest."

No one understands rest better than God. After creating everything, He rested on the seventh day because He wanted to see what He had accomplished. Rest was so important to God that he built days, weeks, and years of rest into the laws of Israel.

In Heaven, you will rest. It will be a good rest. It will be a complete rest. It will be a spiritual rest. It will be God's rest.

DO OUR FAMILY AND FRIENDS MISS US IN HEAVEN AS WE MISS THEM ON EARTH?

I don't believe they do. Heaven would not be Heaven if we experienced the sadness of separation from those we love on Earth. While on the Earth, we miss those who have died. This separation can be unbearable. It can leave a void in our lives. Those closest to us and those important to us—when they die, we miss them. But I don't believe they miss us.

In a church I pastored, I talked with a relative of a person whose funeral service was at the church several years before I arrived. They were very close with this relative, and told me they had tried to attend church, but every time they walked into the sanctuary, they saw the casket in front of the pulpit. They couldn't focus on the service or the sermon. The picture of the casket haunted them to the point they avoided church. I prayed with them that God help them see their relative rejoicing in Heaven. There was no need for them to be haunted by the sight of the casket in the sanctuary. In fact, I prayed they see the same picture as an opportunity to rejoice for their loved one. It took a few years and multiple conversations, but one Sunday I looked out in the congregation and there sat my friend, worshipping God.

I know death can be difficult for those left behind. But death for a believer is a victory, and while we miss those who die, I don't believe they miss us. Let me give you three reasons why:

1. Time as we know it on Earth is different in Heaven. The Bible teaches that with God, a day is like a thousand years, and a thousand years is like a day (2 Peter 3:8). Many scholars believe a twenty-year separation on Earth is a few minutes of separation in Heaven. Do we miss our loved ones? Yes, we do. Do they miss us? Maybe they don't have time to miss us.

2. Believers in Heaven are too busy working (serving God) to miss those on Earth. As I have previously mentioned, I believe work is part of what we will do in Heaven. While God is ruling and reigning over the universe, it's possible that those in Heaven are helping Jesus as he prepares for The Rapture and His Second Coming. There's preparation going on in Heaven, and those in Heaven are a part of it.

3. Believers are too focused on God to miss those on Earth. The primary task of Heaven is worship. Look at what John says:

    > Revelation 7:9, "After this I looked, and there was a vast multitude from every nation, tribe, people, and language, which no one could number, standing before the throne and before the Lamb. They were robed in white with palm branches in their hands."

Here's the good news! One day, His home will be your home. Death is not the end of life. It never has been, and it never will be. Greg Laurie said, "The absence away from our loved ones is a comma, not a period." Death is just the beginning. Billy Graham said, "My home is in heaven. I'm just passing through this world."

Heaven is an actual place because people have gone there and come back to talk about it. It's an actual place because we have assurance that many of our loved ones live there. It is an actual place because God promises to usher you to Heaven by angels when you die (Luke 16:22).

So, to those who say there's no Heaven and there's no life after death, I say, what a horrible way to live. I believe in an eternity with Jesus, who died for me. Why would He die on the Cross, only to let me die at the end of my life? He wouldn't! He died so that I could live eternally with Him. I have faith in another life, a better life, a perfect life for me after I'm dead. I trust in a God who has spoken to me. He has told me Heaven is a real place.

7 Points of Review

1. There are many people who do not believe God is real, nor do they believe Heaven is real. But the apostle Paul says the created world screams the existence of God (Romans 1:20). Since God is real, and the world He created is real, doesn't it make sense that Heaven is real?

2. Right now, Heaven is up there beyond the sky, and beyond outer space. Where? No one knows, but John describes the New Jerusalem as "coming down out of heaven" in Revelation 21:2.

3. Immediate Heaven is temporary because it's not a Christian's final destination. Your final destination is the New Heaven, New Earth, and New Jerusalem described in Revelation 21-22.

4. Immediate Heaven is temporary and eternal. Jesus promises eternal life the moment He saves you, but you will not experience eternal life until you physically die.

5. Joy is better than happiness because happiness in based on the circumstances, but joy is based on Jesus. At the death of a believing loved one, I am sad because they have died, but I am joyous because they are at home in Heaven.

6. There is no one who understands rest better than God. In Heaven, you will rest as you have never rested. It will be a good, complete, and spiritual rest. It will be God's rest.

7. Our family and friends will not miss us in Heaven like we miss them on Earth, because time in Heaven is different from time on Earth.

1. What are the differences between first Heaven, second Heaven, and third Heaven?

   _____

   _____

   _____

   _____

2. Where is Heaven right now?

   _____

   _____

   _____

   _____

3. How is Heaven temporary and eternal at the same time?

   _____

   _____

   _____

   _____

4. What are the three characteristics you will experience in Heaven?

    _____

    _____

    _____

    _____

5. What are the three reasons people in Heaven do not miss their loved ones on the Earth?

    _____

    _____

    _____

    _____

MOTIVATION:

- Think of a time in life when your circumstance was temporary. It could be a temporary job, a relationship, a vacation experience, or a rented home. Describe how you felt.

- How will Heaven differ from your temporary circumstance?

EXAMINATION:

- In Romans 1:20, Paul mentions God's eternal power and His divine nature. Because of this, people are without excuse. Why? Do you agree with what Paul says?

- Heaven is temporary and eternal at the same time. Using John 3:16, Romans 5:21, 6:23, discuss eternal life for the believer on Earth and in Heaven.

APPLICATION:

- Think of a time when you were worshipping God. You were so close to God you were walking in His shadow. How did you feel?

- When we think of Heaven, we focus on the fellowship with our family and friends. But what makes Heaven so perfect is the eternal joy and worship we will have with Jesus. Close this group time by praying and thanking God for His indescribable gift.

CHAPTER THREE: DYING IS NOT DYING, IT'S LIVING

I remember the day, as a pastor, I visited the local hospital. The first visit was to a couple who just gave birth to their first child. There was great joy in their room. Everyone was smiling and laughing. It was an uplifting visit. I prayed with the new family and left full of joy.

From the nursery, I walked to the other end of the hospital, to the Alzheimer's unit. A church member's mother was dying. This dreaded disease had ravaged her mind. There was no excitement, no smiles, and no laughter when I entered the room, just a sense of hopelessness, waiting for what we knew was coming.

After those two visits, I left the hospital and sat in my car for several minutes, drained. In a matter of one hour, I experienced the joy of new life and the sadness of life fading away. This happens on Earth. You're born, then you die. Happiness at birth and sadness at death.

But it doesn't have to be this way. There can be joy at birth and death.

WHY IS DYING NOT DYING FOR THE CHRISTIAN?

John 11 is the story of Jesus raising Lazarus from the dead. Lazarus became very ill, and Mary and Martha, Lazarus' sisters, sent word for Jesus to come and heal their brother. Before Jesus arrived, Lazarus died. Read the following exchange between Jesus and Martha:

> John 11:21-27, "Then Martha said to Jesus, 'Lord, if You had been here, my brother wouldn't have died. Yet even now I know that whatever You ask from God, God will give You.'
>
> 'Your brother will rise again,' Jesus told her.
> Martha said, 'I know that he will rise again in the resurrection at the last day.'
>
> Jesus said to her, 'I am the resurrection and the life. The one who believes in Me, even if he dies, will live. Everyone who lives and believes in Me will never die—ever. Do you believe this?'
> 'Yes, Lord,' she told Him, 'I believe You are the Messiah, the Son of God, who was to come into the world.'"

Jesus tells Martha that anyone who believes in Him, though he dies, he will live. For the Christian, dying is not dying, it's living. The moment you accept Jesus as your Savior, a transformation takes place. You receive a new life, an eternal life. When you receive eternal life, you take on the character of Christ.

How do you die if Christ is living in you? You can't! Dying is not in the cards for a Christian. You simply exchange Earth for Heaven. Paul said in 2 Corinthians 5:8, "to be out of the body is to be at home with the Lord." If God can't die, and God is living in you, then isn't it reasonable that you can't die?

"Neale, what about those funerals where the person lying in the casket is dead?" What died is the physical body, but that's not the most important part of you. God is not just concerned with your body. He is most concerned with your soul and spirit.

We spend most of our time concerned with our body, but very little time concerned with our eternal soul and spirit. America is obsessed with the physical body. There are multiple fitness centers in every city. You can plan your workouts for early morning or late at night. There are many that stay open 24 hours—all to care for the physical body. I admit, it's important, but it's not the most important part of you. Your soul and spirit are more important, because they are the eternal part of you.

So, if you're a Christian and the time comes for you to die, remember, the most important part of you, your soul and spirit, has not died but has been ushered into Heaven, because dying is not dying for the Christian. It's living!

WHY IS IT NECESSARY TO LEAVE OUR EARTHLY BODIES BEHIND?

Do you want to take it with you? If you don't want to take it with you, then you shouldn't mind leaving it behind.

We must leave the earthly body behind because it's only fit for life on Earth. As a believer, you're transformed from a natural body to a spiritual body, from a sinful body to a sinless body, and from a mortal body to an immortal body (1 Corinthians 15:42-53). The Bible tells us it will be like Jesus' resurrected body (1 John 3:2). Here's what I know: What is diseased is healed. What is paralyzed is unparalyzed. What is crooked will become straight.

You must leave your earthly body behind because Paul teaches, on Earth we bear the image of Adam, but in Heaven we will bear the image of Jesus:

> 1 Corinthians 15:48-49, "Like the man made of dust, so are those who are made of dust; like the heavenly man, so are those who are heavenly. And just as we have borne the image of the man made of dust, we will also bear the image of the heavenly man."

Paul says the human body cannot go to Heaven:

> 1 Corinthians 15:50, "Brothers, I tell you this: 'Flesh and blood cannot inherit the kingdom of God, and corruption cannot inherit incorruption.'"

Paul wrote to the Philippian church that a Christian's true citizenship is not on Earth, but in Heaven:

> Philippians 3:20-21, "But our citizenship is in heaven, from which we also eagerly wait for a Savior, the Lord Jesus Christ. He will transform the body of our humble condition into the likeness of His glorious body, by the power that enables Him to subject everything to Himself."

Also, look at what John wrote to believers:

> 1 John 3:2-3, "Dear friends, we are God's children now, and what we will be has not yet been revealed. We know that when He appears, we will be like Him, because we will see Him as He is. And everyone who has this hope in Him purifies himself just as He is pure."

You and I are more than a body. We are body, soul, and spirit. We have the eternal God living in us. Why is God living in us? The Bible gives us three reasons:

First, God is living in us to be the Counselor to help us. When Jesus ascended to Heaven, God sent the Holy Spirit, the Counselor, to be with believers as they live on the Earth. God promises us He will never leave us alone in the world.

> John 14:16-18, "And I will ask the Father, and He will give you another Counselor to be with you forever. He is the Spirit of truth. The world is unable to receive Him because it doesn't see Him or know Him. But you do know Him, because He remains with you and will be in you. I will not leave you as orphans; I am coming to you."

Second, God is living in us to teach us about Jesus. One of the main responsibilities of the Holy Spirit is to teach us the life of Jesus, because it's crucial to our continued growth as a disciple.

> John 14:26, "But the Counselor, the Holy Spirit—the Father will send Him in My name—will teach you all things and remind you of everything I have told you."

Third, God is living in us to guide us to truth and to declare the future. When the Holy Spirit comes, He teaches truth from the past, to the present, and into the future:

> John 16:13, "When the Spirit of truth comes, He will guide you into all the truth. For He will not speak on His own, but He will speak whatever He hears. He will also declare to you what is to come."

When you arrive in Heaven, you will not need the Counselor to help you, because you will have a new spiritual mind full of godly wisdom. When you arrive in Heaven, you're not taught about Jesus. You will be with Jesus. When you arrive in Heaven, you're not guided to truth. Jesus is the Truth, and He is why you are in Heaven. In a nutshell, we must leave our earthly body behind because God has a greater body planned for us in Heaven.

WILL WE HAVE PHYSICAL BODIES IN HEAVEN?

YES! But let me emphasize, it's a temporary body. It's only at the Rapture that you and I receive our new glorified body.

In 2 Corinthians 12:2-4, Paul says he knew a man who was caught up to the third Heaven (Immediate Heaven). He wasn't sure whether the man was in the body or out of the body. Paul was open to the idea while the man was in Heaven, he had a physical body.

But, let's also consider Moses and Elijah, who appeared with Jesus at His Transfiguration (Matthew 17:1-13). The Bible shows they came in the body, not in a spirit. As I read Matthew 17, I always see Jesus, Moses, and Elijah in an actual body. In verse 4, Peter called Moses and Elijah by name. He did so because they were in a body. Later on, in the passage, Jesus and the disciples were discussing Elijah coming, and they believed he came in a body.

Since those in Heaven right now have a physical body, it must be temporary. Look at what Randy Alcorn says in his book, Heaven: "If you are given intermediate forms, they are at best temporary vessels (comparable to the human-appearing bodies that angels sometimes take on), distinct from our true bodies, which remain dead until our resurrection... If Christ's body in the present Heaven has physical properties, it stands to reason that others in Heaven might have physical form as well, even if only temporary ones."

WHY DO JESUS AND PAUL DESCRIBE PHYSICAL DEATH FOR THE BELIEVER AS "SLEEP"?

Jesus said Jairus' daughter was not dead, but only sleeping:

> Luke 8:52, "Everyone was crying and mourning for her. But He said, 'Stop crying, for she is not dead but asleep.'"

The little girl was waiting for Jesus to raise her from the dead. Jesus was correct to refer to her as sleeping. He knew He was going to wake her up and bring her back to life. Was she dead? According to Luke, who was a doctor by profession, she was.

Notice in the following passages, Paul refers to "not dying" as "not sleeping":

> 1 Corinthians 15:51, "Listen! I am telling you a mystery: We will not all fall asleep, but we will all be changed."

> 1 Thessalonians 4:13-18, "We do not want you to be uninformed, brothers, concerning those who are asleep, so that you will not grieve like the rest, who have no hope. Since we believe Jesus died and rose again, in the same way God will bring with Him those who have fallen asleep through Jesus.

For we say this to you by a revelation from the Lord: We who are still alive at the Lord's coming will certainly have no advantage over those who have fallen asleep. For the Lord Himself will descend from heaven with a shout, with the archangel's voice, and with the trumpet of God, and the dead in Christ will rise first. Then we who are still alive will be caught up together with them in the clouds to meet the Lord in the air; and so we will always be with the Lord. Therefore encourage one another with these words."

Six times Paul says, "we" to mean believers, and three times He refers to "sleep" for those believers who died. For the Christians, "sleep" is an excellent metaphor to describe death. The certainty of the resurrection has removed the finality of death. In this passage, the Thessalonians believed those who died would miss the resurrection. Paul corrects them and then gives them a new revelation from God. At the resurrection (Rapture), those who died (asleep) will resurrect first, then those alive will follow them to meet the Lord in the air.

Paul not only gives us a new revelation from God, but he also gives us a truth about death and the Rapture. If you and I are alive when Jesus descends from Heaven to Rapture the church (1 Thessalonians 4:16), guess what we will never experience? That's right, death. When I teach this, you should see the excitement on the faces of those in the audience. Alive at the Rapture? WOW! Somebody has to, and it could be you and me.

What's the one absolute about sleep? You wake up! No one stays asleep forever. Not even Snow White. The same goes for the believer who dies. We don't stay dead; we wake up in Heaven. Physical death for the Christians is not death. It's a change in location. We die on Earth, then we are transformed into Heaven.

WHAT IS "SOUL SLEEP"?

Certain religions believe and teach, as a part of their church doctrine, that after a person dies, their soul "sleeps" until the Rapture. This teaching is not Biblical. The Bible does not say a believer's soul sleeps until the Rapture. Quite the contrary, the Bible is clear: once a believer dies, they go to Heaven.

Those who believe in "soul sleep" teach that when you die, you enter a long unconscious state until the Rapture. This is not what the Bible teaches. Look at what Jesus told the believing thief on the cross:

> Luke 23:43, "And He said to him, 'I assure you: Today you will be with Me in paradise.'"

For further proof, look at the parable of the rich man and Lazarus.

> Luke 16:19-31, "There was a rich man who would dress in purple and fine linen, feasting lavishly every day. But a poor man named Lazarus, covered with sores, was left at his gate. He longed to be filled with what fell from the rich man's table, but the dogs would come and lick his sores. One day the poor man died and was carried away by the angels to Abraham's side. The rich man also died and was buried. And being in torment in Hades, he looked up and saw Abraham a long way off, with Lazarus at his side. 'Father Abraham!' he called out, 'Have mercy on me and send Lazarus to dip the tip of his finger in water and cool my tongue, because I am in agony in this flame!'
>
> 'Son,' Abraham said, 'remember that during your life you received your good things, just as Lazarus received bad things, but now he is comforted here, while you are in agony. Besides all this, a great chasm has been fixed between us and you, so that those who want to pass over from here to you cannot; neither can those from there cross over to us.'
>
> 'Father,' he said, 'then I beg you to send him to my father's house—because I have five brothers—to warn them, so they won't also come to this place of torment.'
>
> But Abraham said, 'They have Moses and the prophets; they should listen to them.'
>
> 'No, father Abraham,' he said. 'But if someone from the dead goes to them, they will repent.'
>
> But he told him, 'If they don't listen to Moses and the prophets, they will not be persuaded if someone rises from the dead.'"

There's two points of view to this story. Many say it's a parable with a central truth. They believe Lazarus and the rich man are not actual people, but they are part of an illustration. While I believe the story is a parable with a central truth, I also believe Lazarus and the rich man are actual people.

In this parable, Jesus gives concrete details he does not give in any other parable. For example, it's the only parable where Jesus mentions a person by their first name. Mentioning Lazarus by name could show Jesus was talking about an actual person. Why did Jesus choose the name Lazarus? There's another man in the Bible named Lazarus, the brother of Mary and Martha, whom Jesus raised from the dead (John 11:1-44). If you're not careful, you could confuse the two men. Why didn't Jesus choose another name, to keep the confusion at a minimum? Maybe because Lazarus is an actual person. If he is, then Jesus is describing what happens to a person when they die.

So, what does Jesus teach regarding a person who dies and goes to Heaven?

1. Angels took Lazarus to Heaven (v. 22). When you die, angels will take you to Heaven.

2. Lazarus went to Abraham in Immediate Heaven.

3. The rich man looked up into Heaven and saw Abraham with Lazarus by his side.

4. There is no indication that Lazarus saw into Torment, but it's debatable since the rich man and Abraham spoke to each other.

5. Lazarus had a finger, and he had a physical body to go with it.

6. Lazarus is in comfort in Heaven, and the rich man is in agony in Torment.

7. There is a chasm between Heaven and Hell, which no one can cross over.

8. As Lazarus was a person on Earth, he was the same person in Heaven.

9. The rich man had a tongue, and again, I'm assuming he had a physical body in Torment.

10. The rich man had memories of his life and family on Earth, even asking Abraham to send Lazarus to warn his brothers.

I believe the purpose of this parable in the Bible is for Jesus to give us a picture of Heaven and Hell. Both are actual places, with people inhabiting each place.

DOES GOD PROMISE YOUNG CHILDREN GO TO HEAVEN WHEN THEY DIE?

YES! The Apostle Paul tells us in Romans 3:23, "For all have sinned and fall short of the glory of God." When Paul says, "all have sinned" he means, "all," including babies and children.

Salvation results from choosing to accept Jesus as your Savior. You're forgiven when you understand you are a sinner. When a child dies before they understand salvation, God's grace and mercy protect them. In the theological world, we call this the "Age of Accountability." The Bible passage used to support this belief is 2 Samuel 12:21-23. This passage is about King David's adultery with Bathsheba, which resulted in Bathsheba becoming pregnant. God sends Nathan to confront David, and tells him, God has determined the child will die. David prayed and fasted, thinking God might change His mind. But once the child died, David ended his prayer and fasting. His actions puzzled his servants, who asked him:

> 2 Samuel 12:21, "What did you just do? While the baby was alive, you fasted and wept, but when he died, you got up and ate food."

David explains his actions:

> 2 Samuel 12:22-23, "While the baby was alive, I fasted and wept because I thought, 'Who knows? The Lord may be gracious to me and let him live.' But now that he is dead, why should I fast?

Can I bring him back again? I'll go to him, but he will never return to me."

David's response shows those who cannot understand salvation are secure with God. David is comforted believing he will see his child again in Heaven.

While "all" sin, God is gracious to protect infants, babies, and children who cannot make the choice to accept Jesus before they die.

If you have experienced the death of an infant child, be comforted. They are in Heaven with Jesus. God always does what's right, and with the "Age of Accountability," this is right.

While you know your child is in Heaven with Jesus, the bigger question is, "Will you be there with them?" Have you accepted Jesus as your Savior?

As we close this chapter, consider the story of Abraham and God's promise to give him an heir from his own body. In Genesis 15:5, God took Abraham outside and told him to look up in the sky and count the stars. God said Abraham's offspring will be like the stars in the sky.

Do you want to know how sure Heaven is? Go outside tonight and count the stars in the sky. Each star is a promise of God. When God makes a promise, He always keeps it. There's not a promise in the Bible that God has not kept or will not keep.

Psalms 19:1, "The heavens declare the glory of God, and the sky proclaims the work of His hands."

Points of Review

1. For the Christian, dying is not dying, it's transforming into a new eternal life. It's exchanging Earth for Heaven.

2. God is not concerned with your body at death, but more concerned with your soul and spirit, because they are the eternal part of you.

3. The destinations of a believer and unbeliever who die are both immediate. The Bible never suggests a holding place after you die.

4. In the New Testament, both Jesus and Paul describe "sleep" as physical death for the believer (Luke 8:52; 1 Corinthians 15:51; 1 Thessalonians 4:13-18). The body sleeps, but the soul and spirit continue to live in Heaven.

5. If you and I are alive when Jesus descends from Heaven at the Rapture, we will never experience death.

6. There is a false-teaching in the world today called "soul sleep." It states that when a believer dies, they enter a long unconscious state until the Rapture. This teaching contradicts the Bible. Note the Scripture passages: Luke 23:43; Revelation 6:9-11; Luke 16:19-31.

7. The story of Lazarus and the rich man is a parable, but it's also about two actual people. In this parable, Jesus gives us concrete details about Heaven and Hell.

5 Big Questions

1. Why is dying not dying for the Christian?

   _____

   _____

   _____

   _____

2. Why is it necessary to leave your earthly body behind when you die?

   _____

   _____

   _____

   _____

3. What do Jesus and Paul teach about death and sleep?

   _____

   _____

   _____

   _____

4. What is "soul sleep," and why is it not biblical?

_____

_____

_____

_____

5. Using Lazarus and the rich man, what does Jesus teach about death and Heaven?

_____

_____

_____

_____

Group Discussion Guide

MOTIVATION:

- Discuss the bookends of life, birth and death. There's excitement at birth and the sadness at death.

- Discuss why dying is not dying for a Christian.

EXAMINATION:

- In John 11:21-26, Jesus and Martha discuss Lazarus' resurrection. Use this passage of Scripture and other passages to discuss God's concern with your soul and spirit at death.

- Using Luke 16:19-31, discuss the ten truths Jesus teaches about life and death. Add your observations to the list.

APPLICATION:

- It's never comfortable to talk about death, especially our own death. If you're afraid of dying, pray and ask God to take away your spirit of fear and give you a spirit of power (2 Timothy 1:7).

- God uses our own experiences to minister to others. Who can you reach out to that has experienced a recent death?

CHAPTER FOUR: HEAVEN AND YOUR RESURRECTION

History has been trying to disprove Christ's Resurrection since the day it happened. The religious leaders of Jesus' day tried everything they could to deny the physical Resurrection of Jesus. They bribed the Roman soldiers who guarded the tomb (Matthew 28:11-15), saying Jesus didn't die, He just passed out (Swoon Theory), then walked out of a sealed and guarded tomb. They even tried to say the women and the disciples went to the wrong tomb. People will do anything to keep the truth from being revealed. Let us clear the air on these theories.

First, if you're going to bribe the soldiers, it's because you have something to hide. You will not bribe a squad of soldiers to tell the truth. No, you want them to lie. That's the very reason you are bribing them. All the religious leaders had to do to disprove the Resurrection and stop Christianity in its tracks two thousand years ago was to produce the dead body of Jesus. If the Resurrection never happened, then why didn't the Jewish leaders and the Roman government produce Jesus' body? They didn't because they couldn't. Why? Because, just as 562 eyewitnesses testified and the Bible records, Jesus rose from the dead.

Second, what about the theory that Jesus didn't die, he just passed out, or he lapsed into a coma? Let's go to the crucifixion. The Roman soldiers at Calvary had one job—nail Jesus and the two thieves to a cross and let them hang there until they were dead. This was not their first crucifixion, and they knew the importance of following through with their duty. If they didn't, they would be derelict, which would result in their own death. That's why the soldier pierced Jesus' side with a spear, and that's why they knew all three victims were dead. If Jesus just passed out, why didn't they bring Him out alive after He recovered for everyone to see?

Third, did the women go to the wrong tomb? No! The Bible tells us that while Joseph and Nicodemus prepared Jesus' body for burial the evening of the crucifixion, Mary Magdalene and the other Mary were sitting across from the tomb (Matthew 27:57-61). The women knew exactly where the tomb was.

Jesus defeated death on the first Easter Sunday morning, and the world has been celebrating His Resurrection every Sunday since. The Resurrection of Jesus is the foundation of Christianity, and Christianity is about a future Resurrection of Christians to Heaven.

WHY IS HEAVEN AND THE RESURRECTION ESSENTIAL TO YOUR FAITH?

You can find the answer in the fifty-eight verses of 1 Corinthians 15. There is no passage in the Bible that speaks as clearly about the Resurrection of Jesus and all believers as 1 Corinthians 15. I believe this powerful chapter gives us six reasons Heaven and the Resurrection are essential to your faith.

1. Heaven and the Resurrection Are Both Cornerstones to the Gospel (vv. 1-11). Paul says the Resurrection is part of the gospel. Christianity is more than the Bible, the Ten Commandments, and the Sermon on the Mount. Christianity is about Jesus Christ resurrecting from the dead and ascending to Heaven. Without a risen Jesus who ascended to Heaven, there is no gospel message. There is no salvation. There is no promise of eternal life. Just look at what Paul writes:

> 1 Corinthians 15:3-4, "That Christ died for our sins according to the Scriptures, that He was buried, that He was raised on the third day according to the Scriptures."

The gospel is about what Jesus did for us. First, He died, a historical fact. Believers and unbelievers agree on this. Second, He was buried. Joseph and Nicodemus testify to it (John 19:38-42), as well as the women, the Roman soldiers, and the Jewish religious leaders. Third, He resurrected. In 1 Corinthians 15, Paul wrote that Jesus appeared to over 500 people at one time. This is the gospel—Jesus died, was buried, and rose again.

The fourth component of the gospel is Heaven. In verse eight, Paul reflects on his personal experience with the resurrected Jesus on the Damascus Road (Acts 9:1-19). Saul (Paul) became a believer when Jesus appeared to him. You and I become believers when Jesus saves us and sends the Holy Spirit to dwell in us. If you don't believe Jesus came from Heaven and returned to Heaven, then you don't believe in the true Jesus from the Bible, because that's what the Bible teaches.

2. Heaven and the Resurrection Are Both Foundations of Christianity (vv. 12-19). In Paul's day, many people did not believe in the Resurrection. They weren't just denying Jesus' Resurrection; they did not believe in any form of resurrection. Paul argues this false belief with a series of "if" statements in 1 Corinthians 15:12-19. Notice what Paul said:

> 1 Corinthians 15:14-15, "If Christ has not been raised, then our proclamation is without foundation, and so is your faith. In addition, we are found to be false witnesses about God, because we have testified about God that He raised up Christ—whom He did not raise up if in fact the dead are not raised."

To summarize, Paul said, if Christ is dead, then preaching has no power, faith has no foundation, and the apostles are liars. But we know the Resurrection is real and Christ is alive. Our faith is genuine, and life does not end at the grave.

Paul's final "if" statement in v. 19 brings Heaven into the picture:

1 Corinthians 15:19, "If we have put our hope in Christ for this life only, we should be pitied more than anyone."

Paul stated there's another life after this one. We know this life is eternal in Heaven.

In his, "Thru The Bible Commentary," J. Vernon McGee said, "May I say Christianity is the here-and-now religion. Paul makes that clear in the sixth chapter of Romans. But Christianity is the hereafter religion. If Christ be not raised, we have been deluded and we are about the most miserable people in the world today. But we're not. We are rejoicing!"

J. Vernon McGee is right. In my personal experience, Christians are the most joyous people on Earth. Why? Because we know this world is not the end. There's another life, a greater life, a better life, a rewarded life with Jesus in Heaven.

3. Heaven and the Resurrection Guarantee Your Resurrection (vv. 20-28).

    Have you ever walked through old cemeteries? You may think, "That's morbid!" Believe it or not, people get a kick out of exploring old cemeteries. I could be one of those people. I preached a funeral for a sweet elderly lady. The chapel service was in Plano, Texas, and then those attending the graveside service made the drive to Oak Hill Cemetery, one of the oldest cemeteries in downtown Dallas. We buried my friend in the old part of the cemetery in a family plot. As I parked and walked to the graveside, I saw gravestones dating as far back as the 1800s.

    As I finished the graveside service, I asked those present to look across the cemetery, and I mentioned the gravestones I passed on my way to the graveside. Then I said, "Imagine Jesus returning to Rapture the church. The grave of every believer in this cemetery will bust open and their body will shoot into the sky to meet the Lord in the air."

    1 Corinthians 15:20-23 reminds us that since Jesus was resurrected, so are believers resurrected. Paul says:

1 Corinthians 15:22, "For as in Adam all died, so also in Christ all will be made alive."

Paul gives an order to this future resurrection of believers. First, comes Jesus' Resurrection. He is the firstfruits (vv. 20, 23). This happened just as the Bible recorded 2,000 years ago. Then comes the resurrection of believers (v. 23). Paul divides this resurrection even further:

1 Thessalonians 4:16 -17, "For the Lord Himself will descend from heaven with a shout, with the archangel's voice, and with the trumpet of God, and the dead in Christ will rise first. Then we who are alive will be caught up together with them in the clouds to meet the Lord in the air and so we will always be with the Lord."

Remember what Jesus said:

John 11:25-26, "I am the resurrection and the life. The one who believes in Me, even if he dies, will live. Everyone who lives and believes in Me will never die, ever. Do you believe this?"

Paul says there's one last enemy God must destroy, and that is the enemy of death (v. 26). Death is an enemy of life. It is not what God intended when He created humanity. But, one day, death will no longer exist on the Earth (Revelation 21:4). Paul said it's been swallowed up in the victory of Jesus' Resurrection and your resurrection (1 Corinthians 15:54-57). It's great knowing that death is not the end of life. God created you to live forever.

4. Heaven and the Resurrection Determine How You Live Life on Earth (vv. 29-34). Many people think that when they get saved, their troubles will cease. I wish that was true. Many times, life gets tougher after salvation. Why? Believers are going against the flow of the world. It's like a salmon swimming upstream. The flow of the world is toward Satan. The flow of the Christian is toward Christ. The flow of the world is self. The flow of the Christian is others. The flow of the world is to gain more. The flow of the Christian is to give more. Do you see the problem? The Christian life contradicts the world.

In verses 29-34, Paul gets sarcastic with the Corinthians because of the things they are doing, and because non-believers are influencing them.

Verse 29 is a complicated verse, but it's connected with what Paul is talking about. Let me try to explain a very controversial verse, and connect it with the Resurrection.

> 1 Corinthians 15:29, "Otherwise what will they do who are being baptized for the dead? If the dead are not raised at all, then why are people baptized for them?"

Whatever Paul is referring to in this verse, he and the Corinthian church understand it. No one else does, but they do. The problem with this verse is that there's no other reference in the Bible that refers to "baptism for the dead." If we take the verse in its context, we can understand it. I believe Paul is talking about the absurdity of believing in the baptism of the dead, yet not believing in the resurrection of the dead. Paul said, "If the dead are not raised at all, then why are people baptized for them?" Paul is frustrated with the Corinthians' lack of belief in the resurrection of believers, and he compares and contrasts it with proxy baptism, a false teaching not found in Scripture.

As Paul stated in v. 30, he knows danger has always been part of the Christian life. He has experienced it firsthand when he had to fight off wild animals in Ephesus using only his hands (v. 32). He goes into great detail about the dangers he's faced in his Christian life in 1 Corinthians 11:23-28.

You and I know the pain and suffering we experience in this life will be worth it when we step into eternity with Christ (Philippians 3:10-14).

The Christian life is knowing there's a resurrection and letting both Heaven and the resurrection determine how we live our life on Earth. If there's no resurrection, live life in the fast lane. Do whatever you want, whenever you want, however you want. But since we know there's a resurrection, live life in the faith lane.

5. Heaven and the Resurrection Transform the Earthly Body into a Heavenly Body (vv. 35-49).

I teach this transformation in chapter two of my book, *All About The Second Coming of Christ*. While I don't have time or space to give you the entire chapter, let me hit several highlights for you:

- You have a body (human) fit for Earth, and you will have a body (spiritual) fit for Heaven.

- The dead in Christ are raised to an actual body, and Paul uses four illustrations to prove it (vv. 36-41).

- R. A. Torrey said, "We will not be disembodied spirits in the world to come, but redeemed spirits, in redeemed bodies, and a redeemed universe."

- There are seven attributes of your new body:

  1. The Holy Spirit controls your heavenly body. You are sown or buried in corruption, sin, weakness, and a natural body. But you are raised or resurrected to incorruption, glory, power, and a spiritual body.

  2. Your heavenly body will be like Jesus' resurrected body (1 Corinthians 15:49; Philippians 3:21; 1 John 3:2).

  3. Your heavenly body is eternal. The Bible promises you, over and over, again and again, eternal life (Matthew 19:29; 25:46; John 3:16, 36; 6:40; 11:25-26; Galatians 6:8; 1 John 5:11, 13).

  4. Your heavenly body will have flesh and bone (Luke 24:39; Job 19:25-27).

  5. Your heavenly body is a glorified body. Many believe it will glow or give off light. Think of Jesus at the Transfiguration (Matthew 17:1-13), or Jesus at Paul's conversion on the Damascus Road (Acts 9:1-9). Also read Daniel 12:3; Matthew 5:14; Philippians 2:14-15.

  6. The new heavenly body will be recognizable. I believe you will be you, the same person you were on Earth, albeit in a new eternal body.

7. Your heavenly body will be unlimited by time, space, and gravity. As Jesus' resurrected body appeared and disappeared at will, you will too.

6. Heaven and the Resurrection Are Victorious Over Death (vv. 50-58). The first heresy in the church was the denial of the bodily resurrection. Throughout 1 Corinthians 15, Paul has shown the truth of Jesus' Resurrection. From the eyewitnesses to his own salvation, Paul argues against the beliefs of his day. He mentions how the dead are raised and the body they will have when they're resurrected. He ends the chapter by declaring victory over death.

In the world, Christ's Resurrection is polarizing. Many believe it without question. Yet others refuse to even examine the overwhelming evidence.

In verses 54-57, Paul uses the word "victory" three times. What's the victory of your resurrection?

First, there's the victory that you're changed at the Rapture:

> 1 Corinthians 15:51-52, "Listen! I am telling you a mystery: We will not all fall asleep (die), but we will be changed, in a moment, in the blink of an eye, at the last trumpet (Rapture). For the trumpet will sound, and the dead will be raised incorruptible (sinless) and we will be changed."

How are you changed? Into the image of Christ (v. 49). Just as you bore the image of the man made of dust (Adam), you will bear the image of the heavenly man (Jesus). Paul says the natural body must come first, then comes the spiritual body (v. 46). The spiritual body is the resurrected body.

Second, there's victory because your death is not the end. In verses 53-54, Paul uses the word "clothed" three times. In the Greek language, the word means "to sink into a garment" or to be "arrayed with clothing." You and I are dressed in incorruptibility and immortality. It's a "must," meaning it's not optional. We cannot go to Heaven in our present earthly natural bodies because they're limited in every way imaginable. We will never experience the greatness of Heaven in our present bodies, so God gives us a new glorious body so that we can enjoy Heaven to the fullest. When you and I get to Heaven, we want to experience everything. For this to happen, we must change from death to life. This is the victory of the resurrection (v. 54). Paul follows this up with two questions: "Death, where is your victory? Death, where is your sting?" (v. 55).

Honestly, I don't fear death. It's not that I want to die, I don't. But I know to die is to go to Heaven, and that is so much greater than the best day of life on this Earth. As I write this, the world is dealing with the COVID-19 virus. We are mandated with social distancing, stay at home orders, wearing masks, and washing our hands. Non-essential businesses are closed, churches are worshipping through online and streaming services. Most everyone is afraid of catching the virus. Maybe I should be, but I'm not. Is the virus real? Yes! Am I afraid? No! Why?

> 2 Timothy 1:7, "For God has not given us a spirit of fearfulness, but one of power, love, and sound judgment."

> 1 John 4:18, "There is no fear in love; instead, perfect love drives out fear, because fear involves punishment."

I don't fear the coronavirus, or the flu, or cancer, or anything that could kill me. If it's my time to die, it's my time to die. When I die, I win.

Third, there's victory because God promises to reward you when you stand firm in the faith. Paul closes the chapter as he began the chapter with a call to stand firm. What a bookend of practical encouragement. In verse 1, Paul proclaims the gospel the Corinthian church received and stood firm that Jesus died for their sins, was buried, and raised on the third day (v. 3-4). In verse 58, he tells the Corinthians to be steadfast, excelling in the work of the Lord, knowing that their work is not in vain, but in victory.

So, 1 Corinthians 15, answers the question of why Heaven and the Resurrection are promised. It teaches the foundations of faith and the cornerstones of Christianity. Both are absolute promises to you.

DOES JESUS' RESURRECTED BODY PROVIDE A MODEL FOR YOUR RESURRECTED BODY?

YES! Here are five verses that note the continuity between your resurrected body and Jesus' resurrected body:

Romans 8:29, "For those He foreknew He also predestined to be conformed to the image of His Son, so that He would be the firstborn among many brothers."

1 Corinthians 15:49, "And just as we have borne the image of the man made of dust, we will also bear the image of the heavenly man."

2 Corinthians 3:18, "We all, with unveiled faces, are looking as in a mirror at the glory of the Lord and are being transformed into the same image from glory to glory; this is from the Lord who is the Spirit."

Philippians 3:21, "He will transform the body of our humble condition into the likeness of His glorious body, by the power that enables Him to subject everything to Himself."

1 John 3:2, "Dear friends, we are God's children now, and what we will be has not yet been revealed. We know that when He appears, we will be like Him, because we will see Him as He is."

Jesus' resurrected body was a real physical body. It had flesh and bone (Luke 24:39). He was touched (Matthew 28:9; John 20:27). He ate food (Luke 24:41-43). He had five senses of sight, sound, smell, taste, and touch (John 21:1-14). His followers recognized him (1 Corinthians 15:5-6). But Jesus' resurrected body was also a spiritual body. He defied gravity (Luke 24:30-31; John 20:19). He glowed and radiated light (Acts 9:3-5; 26:12-15). He ascended into Heaven (Acts 1:9-11).

I believe our resurrected bodies will have many of the same qualities of Jesus' resurrected body. We will have a physical body (Revelation 6:9-11). The martyred saints are given white robes to wear. You will wear a robe on a literal physical body, not on a spirit. We will be flesh and bone (Job 19:26). Job says after he dies, he will see God in a new body of flesh. Paul tells us that our eternal, resurrected body transforms into the likeness of Jesus' glorious body (Philippians 3:21).

I can't think of the Resurrection of Jesus without thinking of Easter Sunday. Let me share a true story I used in a sermon one Easter:

Little Philip, born with Down Syndrome, attended a third-grade Sunday School class with several eight-year-old boys and girls. Typical of that age, the children did not readily accept Philip with his differences. But because of a creative teacher, they began to care about Philip and accept him as part of the group, though not fully.

The Sunday after Easter, the teacher brought L'eggs pantyhose containers, the kind that look like large eggs. Each receiving one, the children were told to go outside on that lovely spring day, find some symbol for new life, and put it in the egg-like container. Back in the classroom, they would share their new-life symbols, opening the containers one by one in surprise fashion. After running about the church property in wild confusion, the students returned to the classroom and placed the containers on the table. Surrounded by the children, the teacher began to open them one by one. After each one, whether a flower, butterfly, or leaf, the class would ooh and ahh.

Then one was opened, revealing nothing inside. The children exclaimed, "That's stupid. That's not fair. Somebody didn't do their assignment." Philip spoke up, "That's mine."

"Philip, you don't ever do things right!" the students retorted. "There's nothing there!"

"I did so do it," Philip insisted. "I did do it. It's empty. The tomb was empty!"

Silence followed. From then on Philip became a full member of the class.

He died not long afterwards from an infection most normal children would have shrugged off. At the funeral this class of eight-year-olds marched up to the altar not with flowers, but with their Sunday school teacher, each to lay on it an empty pantyhose egg.

Those children and their empty eggs remind us that Jesus is alive, and so is their friend Philip.

Every Easter, Christians worldwide, and might I add, every Christian in Heaven, celebrates Jesus' Resurrection from the dead. But Christians celebrate Jesus' Resurrection every Sunday, because every Sunday, we praise and worship a risen Savior.

7 *Points of* **Review**

1. There are many false theories regarding Jesus' Resurrection. All of them try to disprove it. But the fact remains, Jesus rose from the dead. People celebrated it on the first Sunday morning, and the world has been celebrating it every Sunday since.

2. Heaven and Jesus' Resurrection are cornerstones to the gospel. Christianity is about Jesus' Resurrection from the dead and His Ascension into Heaven.

3. Heaven and Jesus' Resurrection are foundations of Christianity. J. Vernon McGee calls Christianity the here-and-now religion and the hereafter religion. If Christ did not rise from the dead, then there's no promise of eternal life. And if there's no eternal life, then there's no Heaven. But Christ rose from the dead. There is eternal life, and there's a Heaven.

4. Heaven and Jesus' Resurrection guarantee your Resurrection. The order of the resurrection is Christ first (v. 20), then believers are resurrected (v. 23). Believers' resurrection is divided even further in 1 Thessalonians 4:16-17, where Paul teaches the dead in Christ are resurrected, then those alive in Christ will follow.

5. Heaven and Jesus' Resurrection determines how you live life on Earth. The Christian life is about knowing there's a resurrection, and letting both Jesus' Resurrection and Heaven determine how we live our life on Earth.

6. Heaven and Jesus' Resurrection transforms the earthly body into a heavenly body. As you have a body fit for Earth, you will have a body fit for Heaven.

7. Heaven and Jesus' Resurrection are victorious over death. The victory at the Rapture will instantly change you. The victory over death will reward you because you stood firm in the faith.

1. According to 1 Corinthians 15:3-4, what is the gospel?

   _____

   _____

   _____

   _____

2. How does Jesus' Resurrection guarantee your resurrection?

   _____

   _____

   _____

   _____

3. Why does life sometimes get harder for a person when they become a Christian?

   _____

   _____

   _____

   _____

4. What are the six attributes of the new heavenly body?

_____

_____

_____

_____

5. What are the victories of your resurrection as mentioned in the chapter?

_____

_____

_____

_____

Group Discussion Guide

MOTIVATION:

- Using a whiteboard or a large piece of paper, brainstorm the facts about Jesus' Resurrection. Try to accumulate a list of ten to twenty items.

- Why do you think the world denies Jesus' Resurrection?

EXAMINATION:

- Discuss the three theories the world uses to deny the Resurrection of Jesus. Before the group discussion, read the gospel accounts of Jesus' Resurrection (Matthew 28; Mark 16; Luke 24; John 20).

- 1 Corinthians 15 is the most comprehensive teaching on the resurrection in the Bible. Use the six reasons given in the chapter to lead your discussion about Heaven and the Resurrection.

APPLICATION:

- Using the list you made at the beginning of the group discussion, pick seven facts that are most important to you. Over the next week, focus on one fact each day, using each one in your prayer time with God.

- Create an outline of Scriptures you can use when you meet a person who does not believe in Heaven and the Resurrection. Make it small enough that you can keep in it your wallet, purse, or in your car. Pull it out and read it weekly to stay fresh.

CHAPTER FIVE: YOU FIT BETTER IN HEAVEN THAN ON EARTH

Have you ever felt like you were in a perfect place? I love to hear people say that they feel they are doing what God created them to do, because it means that they have found their purpose in life. They found where they fit in God's Kingdom.

As a pastor, I want to help Christians discover their spiritual gift, because I believe it helps them find their purpose in life. If you are a Christian, God has given you a spiritual gift. My gift is leadership, but I enjoy teaching the Bible, interceding in prayer for others, and encouraging others. I believe this combination of gifts has helped me find my place in God's Kingdom. I fit as a pastor.

Just as I fit in God's Kingdom on Earth, I will fit even better in God's Kingdom in Heaven. Why do I say that? Because God didn't create me for life on Earth, it's temporary. I believe God created me for life in Heaven, because it's eternal. I have a natural body, fit for life on Earth, but I also have a spiritual body fit for life in Heaven.

When you die and go to Heaven, you will live in a spiritual body. Luke 16, 1 Corinthians 15, Philippians 3:21, 1 John 3:2, and Revelation 6 are just a few of the many passages in the Bible that speak about the new glorious body in Heaven.

WHY DO YOU FIT BETTER IN HEAVEN THAN ON EARTH?

Let me give seven reasons I believe Christians will fit better in Heaven than on Earth:

1. God created us to live forever. The Bible promises eternal life is a gift God gives us for believing in Him. God is eternal, and He created you and me to be eternal, as well.

2. We will live longer on the other side of death. You may live to be one hundred years old on Earth. In eternity, one hundred years is like one day. When the New Heaven and New Earth replace the old Heaven and old Earth, Jesus will usher us into a holy city called the New Jerusalem. This will be our home forever. It will be Heaven on Earth.

3. In Heaven, we will be sinless. When God created humanity, He did so to be sinless. Then Adam and Eve ate the forbidden fruit, and sin came into the world. It has ravaged humanity ever since. In Heaven, there is no sin. So the human body returns to the sinless creation it experienced in the Garden of Eden. We fit better in Heaven because Heaven is sinless, and when we arrive there, so are we.

4. Our Heavenly Father is in Heaven. I don't know if you have a good relationship with your family, but I do. I love my mom and dad and consider them, along with my wife, children, grandchildren, and sisters, as my best friends. I love the time we spend together. Heaven fits like a family because our Heavenly Father lives there, and He is making plans for all His children to live with Him. In this world, as our children get older, they leave home to start their own family, but in Heaven, the opposite happens. In Heaven, the Father comes to live with His children. Why do we fit better in Heaven than

on Earth? Because the family of God lives together in perfect harmony.

5.   Every moment in Heaven is worship to God. I believe every human being is born with a desire to worship. Christians fit better in Heaven because we are there to worship God. Right now, we do that on a limited basis in our human body. But when we get to Heaven, clothed in our spiritual body, it will be natural to worship every moment. I'm not talking about a once-a-week worship service, or even a thirty-minute daily quiet time. I'm talking every moment of eternity. Everything we do, every word we say, every action and reaction we have will be worship of God.

6.   The god of this world is Satan. As Christians, we stand against Satan. We don't fit in the world because we live opposite of the world. Let me give you a couple of examples: The world accepts same-sex marriage, but God teaches that marriage is between a man and a woman. The world teaches to put yourself first, but God teaches to put others first. The world teaches to hate your enemies, but God teaches to love your enemies. Christians fit better in Heaven because we don't have the same beliefs and values as those of the world.

7.   Because God chose us to be "in Christ." Look at what Paul writes in Ephesians:

> Ephesians 1:3-6, "Praise the God and Father of our Lord Jesus Christ, who has blessed us in Christ with every spiritual blessing in the heavens. For He chose us in Him, before the foundation of the world, to be holy and blameless in His sight. In love He predestined us to be adopted through Jesus Christ for Himself, according to His favor and will, to the praise of His glorious grace that He favored us with in the Beloved."

> To be "in Christ" means to be blessed with every spiritual blessing in the heavens (v. 3).

> To be "in Christ" means He chose us before He created the world (v. 4).

To be "in Christ" means we are holy and blameless in His sight (v. 4).

To be "in Christ" means God adopted us through Jesus Christ (v. 5).

To be "in Christ" means we have received God's grace through His beloved Son (v. 6).

WILL YOU BE THE SAME PERSON IN HEAVEN THAT YOU ARE ON EARTH?

Yes, I believe you will be. As you are on Earth, you will be in Heaven, yet without sin. As you enter Heaven at death, God changes you from an earthly being to a heavenly being, but you are still you. When I was born, my parents gave me the name Neale. When I was saved, I was still Neale. When I die, those who know me will remember me as Neale. It will be my name as long as I am on Earth. When I arrive in Heaven, I believe I will be Neale. It's who I've always been, and who I'll always be. Read the names of the Hall of Fame of Faith in Hebrews 11. As they were on Earth, they are in Heaven, absent of sin.

WILL GOD GIVE YOU A NEW NAME IN HEAVEN?

Yes! The Bible shows believers will receive a new name to match their new body they will have in Heaven. In the New Testament, the Apostle John mentions this new name:

Revelation 2:17, "Anyone who has an ear should listen to what the Spirit says to the churches. I will give the victor some of the hidden manna. I will also give him a white stone, and on the stone a new name is inscribed that no one knows except the one who receives it."

Am I contradicting myself? It's possible! But here's what I think. On Earth we are known by our earthly name, and in Heaven we will be known by our heavenly name. Two names are common in the Bible. The Apostle Peter was often called Simon and Peter, and sometimes Simon Peter. The combination name of "Jesus Christ" is mentioned hundreds of times in the Bible. "Jesus" is His earthly name. It's the name the angel told Joseph to name his son (Matthew 1:21). "Christ" is His heavenly name. It defines His deity for eternity. I believe the same is possible for you and me.

But let me add, according to John, the name of God, the name of the New Jerusalem, and the name of Jesus are written on our new bodies:

> Revelation 3:12, "The victor: I will make him a pillar in the sanctuary of My God, and he will never go out again. I will write on him the name of My God, and the name of the city of My God—the new Jerusalem, which comes down out of heaven from My God—and My new name."

If you are critical toward people that have tattoos, rethink that. It's possible you will have a version of a tattoo on your new eternal body forever.

HOW DO YOU GET TO HEAVEN?

As we answer this question, I want you to make two assumptions. First, I want you to assume you are a Christian. You believe Jesus is the Messiah and died on the cross for your sins. And you have confessed and committed your life to Him. I hope you have done this for real, and you don't have to assume you're a Christian. In fact, I pray you know, with complete certainty, that you are a believer in Jesus. Second, I want you to assume tonight, when you go to sleep, you will die. Now, how do you get to Heaven?

First, you get to Heaven by having a personal relationship with Jesus. God promises Heaven is only for believers. Don't believe when everyone dies, they automatically go to Heaven. It's just not true. In eternity, there are only two destinations. Those who believe in Jesus will go to Heaven, but those who do not believe in Jesus will go to Hell. It's that simple!

Part of believing in Jesus is that you must give up yourself and your desires. Why? Because you can't get to Heaven doing your will. You get to Heaven when you accept God's plan for your life. And God's plan is for you to live for Him. When you live for Him, it's a testimony that Christ is living in you. Look at what the Apostle Paul says:

> Galatians 2:19-20, "I have been crucified with Christ and I no longer live, but Christ lives in me. The life I now live in the body, I live by faith in the Son of God, who loved me and gave Himself for me."

The second way you get to Heaven is by angels. In Luke 16, Luke tells us when Lazarus died, angels carried him to Heaven:

> Luke 16:22, "One day the poor man died and was carried away by the angels to Abraham's side."

Paul teaches that the moment you die, you go home to be with God:

> 2 Corinthians 5:6-8, "So, we are always confident and know that while we are at home in the body we are away from the Lord. For we walk by faith, not by sight and we are confident and satisfied to be out of the body and at home with the Lord."

There is no soul sleep, no stop-over place, and no intermediate holding place. At death, you go to Heaven, and angels carry you there.

Let me conclude this chapter with a poem I have used at many funeral services. I believe it speaks of how Christians will fit in Heaven:

IF YOU COULD SEE WHERE I HAVE GONE

If you could see where I have gone the beauty of this place
And how it feels to know you're home to see the Savior's face.
To wake in peace and know no fear just joy beyond compare
While still on earth you miss me yet you wouldn't want me there.

If you could see where I have gone had made the trip with me
You'd know I didn't go alone the Savior came with me.
When I awoke, He was by my side and reached down His hand
Said, "Hurry, you're going home to a grand and glorious land.
Don't worry over those you love for I'm not just with you

And don't you know when you're with me they'll long to be here, too?"

If you could see where I have gone and see what I've been shown
You'd never know another fear or ever feel alone.
You'd marvel at the grace of God his hand on every life
And realize He really cares and bears with us each strife
And that he weeps when one is lost his heart is filled with pain
But Oh the joy when one comes home a child at home again.

If you could see where I have gone could stay awhile with me
Could share the things that God has made to grace eternity.
You would never, ever leave once heaven's joy you'd known
You couldn't bear to walk earth's paths once heaven was your home.

If you could see where I have gone you'd know we'll meet someday.
And though I'm parted from you now I am just away.
And now that I'm home with Him secure in every way
I'm waiting here at heaven's door to greet you some sweet day.

Points of Review

1.   You fit better in Heaven than you do on Earth, because God created you to be eternal and live forever.

2.   You will live longer on the other side of death than on this side of death.

3.   Heaven is a perfect family, because our Heavenly Father lives there, and His children will live there with Him.

4.   You fit better in Heaven because Satan is the god of this world.

5.   In Heaven, you will be the same person you are on Earth, yet without sin. When you die and enter Heaven, God will change you from an earthly being to a heavenly being. But you will still be you.

6.   Heaven and Hell are immediate destinations. Nowhere in the Bible does it indicate an intermediate stop-over, or holding place for those who die.

7.   In the Bible, angels carried Lazarus to Abraham's side (Luke 16:22), and as a believer, angels will carry you into Heaven when you die.

1. Of the promises of Heaven listed in the chapter, which one are you looking forward to the most? Are there other promises you can add to the list?

_____

_____

_____

_____

2. Why do you fit better in Heaven than on Earth?

_____

_____

_____

_____

3. What happens to those who die "in Christ"?

_____

_____

_____

_____

4. Do you believe that the moment you die you go to Heaven? Why do some people believe in an intermediate holding place?

_____

_____

_____

_____

5. How do you get to Heaven?

_____

_____

_____

_____

Group Discussion Guide

MOTIVATION:

- Share a time when you were in the place made for you. You found your purpose. You hit your "sweet spot."

- Describe your personal thoughts about Jesus' greatest promise in John 3:16. What does a promised Heaven mean to you today?

EXAMINATION:

- Discuss with the group why Christians will fit better in Heaven than on Earth.

- Using Luke 16:19-31; 23:43, and 2 Corinthians 5:8, discuss with the group the belief or non-belief in an intermediate hold-over place between Earth and Heaven.

APPLICATION:

- Go outside on a clear night and look at the stars in the sky. Envision Heaven as your home. Praise God that Heaven is real and eternal.

- Challenge yourself over the next three weeks to memorize 1 Corinthians 15:48-49; Philippians 3:20-21, and Revelation 21:4.

CHAPTER SIX: ANGELS: GOD'S HEAVENLY AGENTS

You can't write a book on Heaven and not talk about God's special agents. They are an important part of Heaven. You will find them carrying out God's will throughout the Bible, from Genesis to Revelation.

Angels are mysterious, but the Bible reveals several facts concerning them.

- Angels are spirits (Hebrews 1:14), meaning they are invisible.

- While angels are spirits, they can become visible. Angels appeared to Abraham, Lot, Mary, Joseph, the disciples, and John, just to name a few.

- Angels are neither male nor female. But when they are mentioned in the Bible, it's always in the masculine form. The names Gabriel and Michael are male names.

- An angel's primary purpose is to do God's will as they minister to believers. They serve those who inherit salvation (Hebrews 1:14).

- There are thousands upon thousands, ten-thousand upon ten-thousands of angels (Daniel 7:10; Matthew 26:53; Hebrew 12:22; Revelation 5:11).

- Angels in the Bible are called "Holy Ones" (Psalm 89:5, 7) and "Sons of God" (Job 1:6; 38:7).

- An angel's home is Heaven, but they serve in Heaven and on Earth (Isaiah 6:1-7; Daniel 9:21; Revelation 7:2; 10:1).

- Angels have personality because they have the ingredients of personality, which include intelligence (Luke 1:30-33), emotions (Luke 2:13-14), and will (Jude 6).

- The hierarchy of angels: Archangel - Michael (Jude 9); Special Messenger - Gabriel (Daniel 8:15-16; 9:21-27; Luke 1:11-20, 26-27); Divine Attendants - Cherubim (Ezekiel 1) and Seraphim (Isaiah 6:2-3); Angels of the Church (Revelation 2-3); Angels of Judgment (Revelation 6-20); Fallen Angels - Lucifer (Isaiah 14:12) and a third of the angels.

There is neither time nor space to answer every question about angels from the Bible, but let me pose six questions regarding God's heavenly messengers:

WHEN DID GOD CREATE ANGELS?

Trying to determine the exact time God created the angels is a sticky situation. Many say that God created angels before He created the Earth's foundations. Notice what God said to Job:

Job 38:4-7 (TLB), "Where were you when I laid the foundations of the earth? Tell me, if you know so much. Do you know how its dimensions were determined, and who did the surveying? What supports its foundations, and who laid its cornerstone as the morning stars sang together and all the angels shouted for joy?"

According to Job, the angels praised God as He laid the foundations of the Earth. So, God must have created them before He created the Earth.

Others say God created angels along with everything else during the six-days of creation. They believe the Bible's first verse sets the record straight.

> Genesis 1:1, "In the beginning God created the heavens and the earth."

The phrase "heavens and earth" refers to the entire universe, and this includes all the parts of the universe, including the creation of angels.

So, what does the Bible reveal about the creation of angels? Let's look at two facts:

1. Jesus created angels.

   > John 1:3, "All things were created through Him, and apart from Him not one thing was created that has been created."

   > Colossians 1:16, "For everything was created by Him, in heaven and on earth, the visible and the invisible, whether thrones or dominions or rulers or authorities—all things have been created through Him and for Him."

   Many Bible scholars believe this includes angels.

2. Angels had to be created before the Earth because they worshipped God as He laid the foundations of the world (Job 38:7). The Earth was created on the third day (Genesis 1:10), so God must create angels on the first or second day.

   While we cannot pinpoint the day God created angels, we can know why God created them. The Bible tells us that angels carry out God's will. They are God's messengers or agents.

   > Psalm 103:20 (TLB), "Bless the Lord, you mighty angels of his who carry out his orders, listening for each of his commands."

Psalm 91:11 (TLB), "For he orders his angels to protect you wherever you go."

While angels and their work are mostly unseen on the Earth, I believe when we get to Heaven, we will be amazed to discover the many times God used them to encourage us, guide us, inform us, protect us, and provide for us while we lived on the Earth.

DO CHRISTIANS HAVE A PERSONAL GUARDIAN ANGEL?

The Bible is inconclusive on this issue. Jews developed a belief of a personal guardian angel during the time between the Old Testament and New Testament. Early Jewish scholars believed an individual had a personal angel, and a personal demon. The belief in a guardian angel has been around a long time. Here's the verse many use to support the belief in guardian angels:

Matthew 18:10, "See that you don't look down on one of these little ones, because I tell you that in heaven their angels continually view the face of My Father in heaven."

As I interpret this verse, it's clear that angels serve believers, and they are always watching the face of God so they can hear and respond to God's command when needed. The emphasis is on the angels watching the face of God, not on watching the little ones. Guarding of the little ones seems to come from God, through the angels, which makes logical sense because God is the omniscient Holy One. God sees every believer, and He knows when to send an angel, because they are at His disposal.

There is biblical proof that angels protect us (2 Kings 6:13-17; Daniel 6:20-23), reveal information to us (Luke 1:11-20; Acts 7:52-53), guide us (Matthew 1:20-21; Acts 8:26), provide for us (Genesis 21:17-20; 1 Kings 19:5-7), and minister to us (Hebrews 1:13-14).

I'm not convinced each believer has a personal guardian angel assigned to him or her. As Christians, we have Jesus Christ, who promised never to leave us or forsake us (Hebrews 13:5-6), and we also have the Holy

Spirit, who is our Comforter and Counselor (John 14:16, 15:26). So, why do we need a guardian angel when we have a personal Savior?

DO YOU BECOME AN ANGEL AFTER YOU DIE?

NO! As a pastor, I talk to many people who think when they die and go to Heaven, they become an angel. This is absolutely false. You are a person created in God's image on Earth and that does not change when you get to Heaven. Moses and Elijah are a perfect example. At the Transfiguration in Matthew 17, they were not transformed into angels when they died, but appeared as they were when they lived on Earth, albeit in a heavenly body, and Peter, James, and John recognized them.

The Bible teaches that God created angels with their own histories, memories, identities, and even names—Michael and Gabriel. They are God's special agents that minister to the followers of Christ (Hebrews 1:13-14). There is nothing in the Bible that shows angels were humans on Earth.

There's a primary reason we cannot be angels in Heaven. We return with Christ to the Earth at His Second Coming. We know we will return with Jesus because, 1 Thessalonians 4:17 says, when Jesus raptures us, we will be with Him always. So, when Jesus is on the Earth, we will be there with Him. Angels will live in Heaven, but believers will live with Jesus on the Earth.

Matthew 22:30 is the go-to verse for those who believe humans become angels in Heaven:

> Matthew 22:30, "For in the resurrection they neither marry nor are given in marriage but are like angels in heaven."

But notice Jesus didn't say humans were angels, but only "like" angels, because we are spiritual beings. We need to understand that, in Heaven, angels are angels and humans are humans. While we will not be angels in Heaven, we will be with angels, and that is far better.

DO ANGELS APPEAR TO PEOPLE TODAY?

YES, but on rare occasions. Reading the Bible, one might think angels appearing was common, but that is far from the case. The first appearance of angels in the Bible is Genesis 3:24, when God expelled Adam and Eve from the Garden of Eden. God placed cherubim with a flaming sword to block the entrance. The next appearance of angels in the Bible takes place 1,900 years later, in Genesis 16:7, when Hagar, the mother of Ishmael, was told by an angel to return to Sarai, Abraham's wife. In Genesis 18:2, two angels, along with Jesus, visited Abraham, telling him of the coming destruction of Sodom and Gomorrah. The same two angels visited with Lot in Genesis 19:1-11, telling him to take his family and flee the city before it's destroyed.

In Genesis 32:1, Jacob saw a multitude of angels he recognized as the army of God. In Numbers 22:22, an angel confronted the disobedient prophet, Balaam. He didn't see the angel at first, but his donkey did. In Luke 1, the angel Gabriel predicts John's birth (vv. 5-25), and Jesus' birth (vv. 26-38). In Matthew 2:13, an angel warned Joseph to take Mary and Jesus and flee to Egypt.

Angels deliver messages from God by supernatural means to point people to God. According to modern day reports, angelic appearances come in various forms. People report a stranger arriving to prevent a serious injury or potential death and then disappearing. The elderly report feeling arms, even wings, wrapped around them in times of great loneliness. The Bible speaks of God covering His children with His wings.

> Psalm 91:4, "He will cover you with His feathers; you will take refuge under His wings. His faithfulness will be a protective shield."

A third visitation involving an angel is the report of winged or white-clothed beings who appear and then vanish. People who encounter angels feel peace and assurance from the angel's appearance. Notice Paul's encounter with an angel:

> Acts 27:23-24, "For this night an angel of the God I belong to and serve stood by me, and said, 'Don't be afraid, Paul. You

must stand before Caesar. And, look! God has graciously given you all those who are sailing with you.'"

My son, Roger, had a similar experience with an angel on two different occasions. Here's his story:

"My wife, Ashton and I had been married for 7 or 8 months when I woke up one night and saw an Angel at the foot of our bed. I knew immediately, this was an Angel. Don't ask me how I knew, I just knew. The Angel wore a white robe that was dazzling. It was blinding, but it did not illuminate the room. It felt like I was looking at an LED light. The robe had a hood that covered his head, and the only part of the Angel I could see was his face and hands, which were the same color as the robe. I could not see any facial features because of his brightness.

After looking at the Angel, I blinked. I wanted to make sure what I was seeing was real. As I blinked, the Angel disappeared from the outside inward, and completely disappeared in five or six seconds.

Today, as I reflect on the Angel's appearance, I remember feeling a peace that I had never felt before. You might think seeing an Angel in the middle of the night would be very frightening, but I wasn't. I remember thinking about it for a few minutes and then quietly going back to sleep.

It was about a week and a half later; I had another encounter. I woke up in the middle of the night and there was a second Angel, in the same spot, at the foot of the bed. This Angel was wearing the same bright white robe, but this time, his face and hands were dark. Could it be Angels have different skin-tones, just as humans do?

Like the first encounter, I felt the same peaceful feeling come over me. I blinked, thinking the Angel would disappear, as he did before, but that didn't happen. Now, the Angel and I were looking at each other. This continued for a few seconds until I rolled over on my stomach, thinking that when I rolled back over, he would be gone. So, that's what I did. I counted to three, and as soon as I hit three and started turning over, I felt a hand touch my right leg, halfway up my calf. It was a soft touch, like one you would give to someone you are praying for.

Now, I was on my stomach and I felt a rush of adrenaline which I'd never felt before. It was like my heart was going to burst out of my chest. That peaceful feeling disappeared, and now fear suddenly overwhelmed me.

Ashton and I have a reading light above our bed. So, I counted to three one more time, turned on the light, and rolled over, but by this time he had disappeared. I woke Ashton up as I was trying to catch my breath. She just looked at me, confused, as if I'd had a nightmare. But this was no nightmare. This was real. I told her I was fine and to go back to sleep. Unlike the first time, I had a harder time falling asleep.

I didn't tell Ashton about my experiences for five years, because I thought it might scare her. I wondered what these encounters meant, and I knew she would, too. Why would God allow me to see two Angels? Why did the second Angel touch me? Did the touch mean something specific?

When I told Ashton about these appearances, her reaction surprised me. She wasn't scared. Naturally, she had questions, but she was very supportive and never doubted that my experiences were real.

It took me a few more years before I was comfortable telling my family. I'm sure they had their doubts. Who wouldn't! If it hadn't happened to me, I would have doubts. You may read this and have doubts yourself. I don't need anyone to believe me. I know I saw two Angels and I know it was real. Maybe that's why God sent the second Angel. All these years later, it might be easy to dismiss the first encounter. It happened so quickly. But the second one, there's no denying that one. The touch and the adrenaline rush I experienced still overwhelm me today.

What message was God trying to send me through these two Angels? Was he just letting me know He is real and Angels are real? Possibly. But I'm convinced there is more to it. There is a reason the Angel touched me. It was not an accident. I still don't have all my questions answered, but I believe my encounters with the Angels was God telling me He loves me and cares for me very much, and that He has His Angels watching over me. I believe the Angels have given me a strength or a symbol of strength that I will need one day. When that will be, I don't know.

God teaches me about my Angel encounters every time I speak or write about it. Even now, as I write this, God is teaching me. With each opportunity, God continues to reveal Himself to me as I continue to walk with Him.

I hope my experiences inspire you. I know Angels are real. They watch over us and intercede for us, more than we think. Since Angels are real, the One who created them is real, and that is something I will never doubt, especially after these two encounters."

Hebrews 13:2 (TLB) reminds us, "Don't forget to be kind to strangers, for some who have done this have entertained angels without realizing it!"

WHY ARE BELIEVERS "NOT" TO WORSHIP ANGELS?

In Revelation 22:8, John repeats an earlier mistake he made in Revelation 19:10 when he bowed down before the angel. Why did John do this again? He was overwhelmed, just as he was in 19:10. But, this could also be a sign that it's difficult for humans to distinguish between angels and deity.

John is clear we are not to bow to angels. Why? The angel answers the question when he tells John he is a fellow servant with John and all other believers (Revelation 22:9). But the Bible gives us another reason we are not to bow down before angels. In Heaven, we have a higher position than angels. God created us in His image, and Christ redeemed us (Luke 1:68; Galatians 3:13; 1 Peter 2:9). God did not create angels in His image, nor did Christ redeem them. The Apostle Paul gives us a picture of the higher position:

> 1 Corinthians 6:2-3, "Or do you not know that the saints will judge the world? And if the world is judged by you, are you unworthy to judge the smallest cases? Do you not know that we will judge angels—not to mention ordinary matters?"

The Greek word "judge" means to "rule or govern." I believe what Paul is stating in these verses is two-fold:

First, the angels we judge are the fallen angels. God threw them to the Earth with Satan:

Revelation 12:4, "His tail swept away a third of the stars in heaven and hurled them to the earth."

A third of the stars refers to one-third of the angels that fell with Satan to the Earth. They are chained until the judgment:

2 Peter 2:4, "For if God didn't spare the angels who sinned, but threw them down into Tartarus and delivered them to be kept in chains of darkness until judgment."

Jude 6, "And He has kept, with eternal chains in darkness for the judgment of the great day, the angels who did not keep their own position but deserted their proper dwelling."

Second, just as Christ is exalted over the angels (Ephesians 1:20-23), believers who reign with Him share His authority, even over angels.

2 Timothy 2:12, "If we endure, we will also reign with Him."

Revelation 20:4 (MSG), "I saw thrones. Those put in charge of judgment sat on the thrones. I also saw the souls of those beheaded because of their witness to Jesus and the Word of God, who refused to worship either the Beast or his image, refused to take his mark on forehead or hand—they lived and reigned with Christ for a thousand years!"

Angels are messengers sent by God. They were in biblical days, and they are today. While we don't see angels as active in believer's lives, because we have the indwelling of the Holy Spirit, they are active in many non-believer's lives, calling them to come to Christ. There are reports coming out of the Middle East of people raised Muslim that have experienced visions or dreams with angels who call them to seek faith in Jesus. The angel in the dream instructs them, the same way Jesus instructed Saul in Acts 9, to go to a certain place, or seek a certain person. Angels were sent by God in the days of the Bible, and God still sends them today. They have a divine purpose as messengers of God. But John states that they are not to be worshipped.

WHAT DO ANGELS DO FOR CHRISTIANS TODAY?

There are many things which happen in the world today that can only be explained by angels. They are very real and necessary in the world. While the Bible is clear that we are not to worship angels, it's also clear that we need angels. As I have studied angels in the Bible, I see four ministries angels perform for born-again believers:

1. Angels reveal God's will to believers. Remember, the sole purpose of angels is to carry out God's will, and they do that by following the orders God gives them (Matthew 4:6). In Matthew 1:20, it was an angel that appeared to Joseph in a dream and told him it was God's will for Joseph to take Mary as his wife. Then the angel explained Mary was to be the mother of the Messiah. In v. 24, Joseph got up from sleeping, and did as the angel commanded him. In Matthew 2, an angel appeared to Joseph again, revealing God's will to take Mary and Jesus and flee to Egypt, for King Herod wanted to kill the child. In Acts 8:26, it was an angel that took Philip to Gaza. There he found an Ethiopian man. The Holy Spirit led him to his chariot (v. 29), and Philip led the man to faith in Jesus. As God does for Joseph and Philip, and others in the Bible, He also does for you and me.

2. Angels encourage believers. In Matthew 4, the Devil tempts Jesus in the wilderness. In the Devil's second temptation, he took Jesus to the pinnacle of the temple and challenged Jesus to throw Himself down. If He did, God would give the angels orders concerning Jesus. After the third temptation, Matthew 4:11 says, "Then the Devil left Him, and immediately the angels came and began to serve Him." These angels encouraged Jesus after His temptation with the Devil.

3. Angels protect believers from physical and spiritual harm. That's what Psalm 91:11 says, "For He will give His angels orders concerning you, to protect you in all your ways." In John 10:10, Jesus says the Devil wants to kill, steal, and destroy God's children. We are in physical and spiritual danger against the Enemy every day. If Satan could, he would end your life. John 8:44 says that Satan is a murderer and has been from the beginning. The reason he wants

to kill is to keep people from coming to faith in Jesus. If you're a believer, Satan wants to kill you to keep you from being a witness to Jesus. But God sends His angels to protect you. We may never know how many times angels protected us from the Devil and his demons.

4. Angels minister to believers in their death. In Luke 16, we have the story of the rich man and Lazarus. The rich man died and was buried. Lazarus, the poor man died, and the Bible says angels carried him away to Abraham's side (Heaven). We know that death can be frightening because it's the great unknown. But a Christian should not fear death. When we close our eyes for the last time on Earth, we will see angels, and they will usher us into an eternity with Jesus in Heaven. We know death is not a pleasant event. My family and I understand that, having lost my mom and dad within ten-days. While we hurt, we are happy, because we know they are healthy in Heaven with Jesus. Death for the Christian is not the end of life, it's the beginning of life. In fact, Revelation 14:13 says, "Blessed are the dead who die in the Lord from now on."

ARE SATAN AND HIS DEMONS FALLEN ANGELS?

Ezekiel 28:12-18 describes Satan as a "guardian cherub." Many theologians believe this passage to be a symbolic description of Satan. Cherubs are angels of the highest order. So, does this make Satan an angel? Yes, I believe it does.

Job 1:6-7 says that Satan came before the LORD with the "sons of God" (angels). Matthew 25:41 mentions the Devil and his angels. Revelation 12:7 describes the war in Heaven and says Michael, an archangel, and his angels fought against the Dragon (Satan) and his angels. From these passages, it's clear that Satan was an angel who rebelled against God. For that, God cast him out of Heaven to the Earth.

Why did Satan rebel against God? According to Isaiah 14:12-14 (another symbolic passage), Satan rebelled because of pride. Satan was the most beautiful and powerful of all the Cherubs, but that wasn't good enough for him. He wanted to be God. Satan didn't want to worship God, he wanted to be worshipped as God. So, Satan rebelled and took a group of angels with him.

How many angels fell with Satan? It's accepted that one third of the angels fell from Heaven. Revelation 12:3-4 describes Satan's fall from Heaven, and Revelation 12:7-9 describes a war in Heaven. A third of the stars swept away by the Dragon's tail are the angels. After the war in Heaven, God throws the Dragon, also called the ancient serpent, the Devil, and Satan, to the Earth along with his angels.

One of the significant stories about angels is the story of John Paton, a missionary in the New Hebrides Islands: One night, hostile natives surrounded the mission station, intent on burning out the Patons and killing them. Paton and his wife prayed during that terror-filled night that God would deliver them. When daylight came, they were amazed to see their attackers leave. A year later, the chief of the tribe was converted to Christ. Remembering what had happened, Paton asked the chief what had kept him from burning down the house and killing them. The chief replied in surprise, "Who were all those men with you there?" Paton knew no men were present—but the chief said he was afraid to attack because he had seen hundreds of big men in shining garments with drawn swords circling the mission station.

What a beautiful story of God sending His angels to protect the Patons. As God did for them, He also does for you and me.

Points of Review

1. Angels are spirits, meaning they are invisible. But while they are spirits, they can become visible. Angels appeared to many people in the Bible, and people today have reported seeing angels.

2. An angel's primary purpose is to do God's will as they minister to believers.

3. We know angels had to be created before the Earth because they worshipped God as He laid the foundations of the world (Job 38:7).

4. The Bible is inconclusive on the belief that every believer has a guardian angel.

5. Christians do NOT become angels after they die. In Heaven, angels are angels, and humans are humans. While Christians do not become angels in Heaven, they will be with angels, and this is far better.

6. Angels appear to people today on rare occasions. Hebrews 13:2 reminds Christians to be kind to strangers, because they may entertain an angel.

7. It's accepted in Christian theological circles that Satan and demons are fallen angels.

1. Why did God create angels?

_____

_____

_____

_____

2. Why do believers not need a personal guardian angel?

_____

_____

_____

_____

3. Why do Christians not become an angel after they die?

_____

_____

_____

_____

4. Why did Satan rebel against God?

_____

_____

_____

_____

5. What are the four ministries that angels perform for Christians today?

_____

_____

_____

_____

Group Discussion Guide

MOTIVATION:

- How would you describe the entertainment industry's depiction of angels in movies and on television?

- How does this differ from what you know about angels in the Bible?

EXAMINATION:

- When and why did God create angels?

- Using the information in the chapter, discuss what angels do for Christians today.

APPLICATION:

- Do a personal study of angels. Read every passage in the Bible where angels appear. See if you can discover similar facts about each appearance.

- Has there been a time when you believed there was an angelic presence in your life? If so, record it on paper with as much details as you can remember.

PART TWO:
ETERNAL HEAVEN

(THE PLACE YOU WILL LIVE FOREVER)

REVELATION 21-22

CHAPTER SEVEN: WHERE EVERYTHING IS NEW

I don't know about you, but I like new stuff. New clothes. New shoes. New furniture. Even a new home. But, for me, nothing is better than a new car (a slightly used car). When I get a new car, I keep the exterior washed, and the interior detailed.

If you're like me, you want to keep your stuff new as long as possible, and my car is no exception. But no matter how hard I try, it's just not going to stay new forever. Eventually, my new car will become my old car. It's just a fact.

Everything on Earth is deteriorating. Nothing will last forever. Everything will die. Drive around your community and look at the neighborhoods that fifty years ago were the places to live, and today, they have become run-down houses. You don't see too many 1966 Ford Mustangs in prime condition. Most are rusting away in the junkyard. Nothing on this Earth will last forever. Not even you. You are aging, and one day you will die.

But, if you believe in Jesus, there's coming a day when you will step into a New Heaven and onto New Earth, and you will live in the New Jerusalem. It's going to be completely different from the present Earth. Look at what John writes about this new place.

Revelation 21:1-8, "Then I saw a new heaven and a new earth, for the first heaven and the first earth had passed away, and the sea existed no longer. I also saw the Holy City, new Jerusalem, coming down out of heaven from God, prepared like a bride adorned for her husband. Then I heard a loud voice from the throne, 'Look! God's dwelling is with men, and He will live with them. They will be His people, and God Himself will be with them and be their God. He will wipe away every tear from their eyes. Death will exist no longer; grief, crying, and pain will exist no longer, because the previous things have passed away.' Then the One seated on the throne said, 'Look! I am making everything new.' He also said, 'Write, because these words are faithful and true.' And He said to me, 'It is done! I am the Alpha and the Omega, the Beginning and the End. I will give to the thirsty from the spring of living water as a gift. The victor will inherit these things, and I will be his God, and he will be My son. But the cowards, unbelievers, vile, murderers, sexually immoral, sorcerers, idolaters, and all liars—their share will be in the lake that burns with fire and sulfur, which is the second death.'"

WHY DOES THE FIRST HEAVEN AND FIRST EARTH PASS AWAY?

Revelation 21:1 says the first Heaven and first Earth pass away, but the Bible says the Earth will last forever.

Psalm 78:69, "He built His sanctuary like the heights, like the earth that He established forever."

Psalm 104:5, "He established the earth on its foundations; it will never be shaken."

Ecclesiastes 1:4, "A generation goes, and a generation comes, but the earth remains forever."

Is there a contradiction? No! When John saw a New Heaven and a New Earth, he saw "new" in quality. Solomon was right when he said, the Earth will last forever. But not in its present form. It will return to its original creation before sin corrupted it in Genesis 3. Before Adam and Eve sinned, the Earth was pristine and perfect. It was sinless and sacred. That's the New Earth you will inhabit.

The first Heaven and first Earth must "pass away," because fire must refine and purify the Earth. Look at what Peter said:

> 2 Peter 3:10-13, "But the Day of the Lord will come like a thief; on that day the heavens will pass away with a loud noise, the elements will burn and be dissolved, and the earth and the works on it will be disclosed. Since all these things are to be destroyed in this way, it is clear what sort of people you should be in holy conduct and godliness as you wait for and earnestly desire the coming of the day of God, because of which the heavens will be on fire and be dissolved, and the elements will melt with the heat. But based on His promise, we wait for new heavens and a new earth, where righteousness will dwell."

The first Heaven and first Earth must "pass away," because Satan is the god of it.

> 2 Corinthians 4:4, "The god of age has blinded the minds of unbelievers so they cannot see the light of the gospel of the glory of Christ."

> Ephesians 2:1-2, "And you were dead in your trespasses and sins in which you previously walked according to the ways of this world, according to the ruler who exercises authority over the lower heavens, the spirit now working in the disobedient."

Satan's ideas, opinions, and views have influenced most people in the world (Matthew 7:13). He's created false religions under his control to counteract God's true word. While Satan influences the world, he doesn't rule the world. God is omniscient, omnipotent, and omnipresent. But in God's infinite wisdom, He has allowed Satan to influence unbelievers. It's important to know Satan has no power over believers.

> Colossians 1:13-14, "He has rescued us from the domain of darkness and transferred us into the kingdom of the Son He loves. We have redemption, the forgiveness of sins, in Him."

Jesus tells us that Satan will be cast out of the world (John 12:31). His influence will vanish and vaporize in the refining and purifying fire of God's New Heaven and New Earth.

WHY IS THERE A NEW ARRANGEMENT OF WATER ON THE NEW EARTH?

Let's take into consideration a couple of things, as John writes in Revelation 21. First, he is in prison on the island of Patmos, and everywhere he looks, all he sees is water. Since there is no sea in Heaven, he will not miss this detail. Second, The Jews had a fear of the sea. They believed if a person died at sea, they could not be resurrected, and would be lost forever. The Jews believe the sea was inherently evil, and evil spirits from Satan caused storms. So, John writing there's no sea in Heaven would have comforted his readers.

What does John mean when he says, "and the sea existed no longer"? I don't believe he meant there will not be large bodies of water on the New Earth. I believe there will be. My family's annual vacation is to rent a beach house on Galveston Island, Texas, and just be beach bums for a week. In eternity, I believe there are beaches and water, just as I believe there are mountains and deserts. The different climates we have on present Earth we will have on the New Earth, but in its purest form.

The current arrangement of water, that occupies three-fourths of the present Earth, will not be necessary. I believe there will be lakes, rivers, and smaller versions of oceans on the New Earth. These bodies of water will not be necessary to sustain life, but will be for beauty and pleasure as we glorify God. Remember, everything on the New Earth will be to worship and praise God, even the water.

Why are there no more seas? I believe it's because the entire world is inhabited. Many scientists believe that at one time the continents were connected. Bible scholars agree, and date the continents connecting to before the flood and Noah's Ark (Genesis 7-9). If the Earth returns to its pre-flood condition, then the continents will once again connect.

WHAT DOES JOHN MEAN WHEN HE SAYS THE HOLY CITY IS, "COMING DOWN OUT OF HEAVEN FROM GOD"?

John means that, while this city is built in Heaven, it's meant for the New Earth. I have taught in the past that the Holy City, the New Jerusalem, was suspended above the Earth, and Christians traveled back and forth between the two. I no longer believe this. I'm convinced the Holy City is on the New Earth. It's important to understand this Holy City is an actual city, and not a state of mind or a figment of your imagination. It is being prepared by Jesus right now (John 14:1-3). The Holy City will descend from Immediate Heaven and reside on the New Earth.

When it descends from Heaven to Earth, it's the merging of two realms. Heaven and Earth, now separated, are joined in a New Heaven and New Earth. The chasm between the spiritual world and physical world dissolves. It's rolled back as if it never existed. There will be no divided realms, only one universe, ruled by one Messiah, forever.

WHY DOES GOD LIVE ON THE NEW EARTH?

Today, God lives in Heaven. When you and I die, we go to where God is, Immediate Heaven. In eternity, God will come to the New Earth and live with us. Why does God live with us? So, we can have access to Him. Today, we do not have face-to-face access to the Heavenly Father. We have the Holy Spirit dwelling in us, but we do not have personal access to the Father. That will change in eternity. We will see Him, walk with Him, eat with Him, have fellowship with Him. We will live with Him just as we live with other believers, and it will be for eternity. We will have the same fellowship with the Father that Adam and Eve had in the Garden of Eden, yet better, because He will live with us on the New Earth.

At Christmas, we often recite two passages of Scripture, one from the Old Testament and one from the New Testament. One is a prophecy, the other is a reality.

Isaiah 7:14, "Therefore, the Lord Himself will give you a sign: The virgin will conceive, have a son, and name him Immanuel."

Matthew 1:23, "See, the virgin will become pregnant and give birth to a son, and they will name Him Immanuel, which is translated 'God is with us'."

It took seven hundred years for the prophecy to become a reality. Jesus fulfilled Isaiah's prophecy by becoming "God with us!" Jesus came to live in Israel with His people, just as Isaiah foretold. The Gospel of John tells us of the Immanuel:

John 1:14-18, "The Word became flesh and took up residence among us. We observed His glory, the glory as the One and Only Son from the Father, full of grace and truth. (John testified concerning Him and exclaimed, 'This was the One of whom I said, The One coming after me has surpassed me, because He existed before me.') Indeed, we have all received grace after grace from His fullness, for although the law was given through Moses, grace and truth came through Jesus Christ. No one has ever seen God. The One and Only Son—the One who is at the Father's side—He has revealed Him."

At Jesus' First Coming, He came to die on a cross. At Jesus' Second Coming, He comes to conquer Satan and sin, and set up His Kingdom on the Earth. The only thing better is when God, the Father, comes to live with us on the New Heaven and New Earth forever. Jesus' coming was temporary, but the Heavenly Father's coming is permanent. John tells us in Revelation 21:3, God is the Immanuel. He is with us in person. As great as eternal Heaven will be, it will never overshadow the Immanuel.

WHAT WILL NOT BE IN HEAVEN?

The only way John could describe the new creation was by the contrast of "no more." In eternity, the things of this life have passed away (departed, vanished, died). Notice the characteristics of your life in the New Heaven:

- No more death. The Bible represents death as separation. It results from sin (Romans 6:23). It's man's greatest valley because it's the fear of the unknown. Death reminds us of our own mortality. It leaves an empty void in our hearts when a loved one dies.

  There is physical death (first death) and spiritual death (second death). Creation is subject to death because all have sinned.

  > Romans 5:12, "Therefore, just as sin entered the world through one man, and death through sin, in this way death spread to all men, because all sinned."

  God created man to be sinless and perfect. Death came because of the Devil. On the cross, Jesus defeated death and proved it when He resurrected three days later.

  > 1 Corinthians 15:21-22, 26, "For since death came through a man, the resurrection of the dead also comes through a man. For as in Adam all die, so also in Christ all will be made alive... The last enemy to be abolished is death."

  For the unsaved, death ends any chance of accepting God's gracious gift of salvation. For the saved, death brings us into God's presence. John reminds us believers are promised a time when "Death will no longer exist" (Revelation 21:4).

  In eternal Heaven, death is erased, eradicated, and evaporated. It's defeated. There will be no graves, tombstones, cemeteries. There will be no funeral homes or funeral directors to counsel grieving families. In eternity, death is a non-existent memory. No one will ever carry another casket to a grave.

  > 1 Corinthians 15:55, "Death, where is your victory? Death, where is your sting?"

- No more grief. Grief is a deep emotion caused by the death of someone very dear to us. If you live long enough on this Earth, you will experience grief. Why? Because death is a part of life. There are many sources of grief on Earth. But death may be the greatest. John reminds us there's no hint of grief anywhere in Heaven. The things that cause despair on the Earth disappear in Heaven. That which causes disappointment on Earth is dissolved in Heaven. And the things that cause discouragement on Earth are defeated in Heaven. There is no grief of separation from a saved loved one because you are with each other for eternity.

- No more crying. Crying often comes from grief. There are tears at the death of someone you love. At the loss of a job. At the betrayal of a friend. A quick study of the word "crying" in the Bible shows:

  The children of Israel crying out in misery from their oppressors.

  Exodus 3:7, "Then the Lord said, "I have observed the misery of My people in Egypt, and have heard them crying out because of their oppressors, and I know about their sufferings."

  David was weary from crying.

  Psalm 69:3, "I am weary from my crying; my throat is parched. My eyes fail, looking for my God."

  The Gadarene Demoniac cried out in the tombs and cut himself.

  Mark 5:5, "And always, night and day, he was crying out among the tombs and in the mountains and cutting himself with stones."

  Jesus cried at the death of Lazarus.

  John 11:35, "Jesus wept."

  John cried because no one was worthy of opening the scroll.

  Revelation 5:4, "And I cried and cried because no one was found worthy to open the scroll or even to look in it."

  John reminds us that God will wipe away every tear from our eyes. In Heaven, there's no crying over death or divorce or defeat. In eternal Heaven, you will never cry another tear, ever!

- No more pain. Pain means suffering. In this life, pain is not something we want, but it's something we expect. One little instance of pain can sink a boatload of joy. Pain teaches us how weak we are. It distracts our minds and destroys our body. It makes life tedious and weary. Pain can be chronic. It can be terminal. Pain can result from a broken heart. I can't think about pain without thinking about the torturous pain Jesus went through on the cross. But here's the good news: in eternal Heaven, there's no pain. Chronic pain from a birth defect—Gone! Physical pain from a car wreck—Gone! Emotional pain from a broken relationship—Gone! Psychological pain from a life of selfish choices—Gone! Even spiritual pain from a life of sin—Gone! Pain in Heaven is non-existent, and I believe the memory of pain will also be non-existent.

WHO ARE THE VICTORS?

The victors are the ones who believe that Jesus is the KING OF KINGS AND LORD OF LORDS. Jesus says the victor will inherit the New Jerusalem. Today, when a person inherits property, they become the owner. When you inherit the New Jerusalem, you will not just live there, you will own it.

God will be your Heavenly Father, and you will be His heavenly child. With this in mind, let me offer five characteristics of the victors:

1. Faith: The victor overcomes the world, and that can only happen by faith in Jesus Christ.

2. Awareness: The victor must know his, "Adversary, the Devil is prowling around like a roaring lion looking for anyone he can devour" (1 Peter 5:8).

3. Prayer: Who can be victorious over the Devil if they are not a person of passionate prayer? Prayer is a necessary weapon in defeating the Devil.

4. Humility: Pride is a problem for most everyone on Earth. Humbling oneself is not admitting we are weak, but acknowledging He is strong. When we humble ourselves we are denying ourselves and coming to the throne of God.

5. Perseverance: Let's face it, it's difficult to be a Christian in the world today. The world attacks us from every direction. The Apostle Paul

tells us, after putting on the armor of God, to pray, stay alert, and persevere.

Be sure you're saved because the next verse is a group of sinners that will not be in the New Heaven or on the New Earth.

WHO ARE THOSE THAT ARE BANNED FROM ETERNAL HEAVEN?

John goes from telling you who will be there to telling you who will not be there. He expands the list of the ungrateful eight in Revelation 21:27 and then repeats it in Revelation 22:15. Their judgment is the Lake of Fire, the "second death." So, who is overcome by sin and banned from eternal Heaven?

1. Cowards: They refuse to stand up for Jesus and do not have the courage to profess faith in Him, so they serve Satan.

2. Unbelievers: They reject Jesus' offer of salvation. They hear the gospel, but choose not to believe. Jesus said, "For if you do not believe that I am He, you will die in your sins" (John 8:24).

3. Vile: They practice wickedness, polluting themselves in their mind, spirit, and body by worshipping Satan. They are spiritually filthy.

4. Murderers: They kill the saints. Specifically, the saints of the Tribulation Period (Revelation 6: 9-11). It is a solemn thing to kill God's supreme creation, a human life.

5. Sexually immoral: They practice fornication, adultery, and perverse sex. They ruin another person's physical virtue.

6. Sorcerers: They practice witchcraft, spells, spiritualism, devil worship, and other forms of sorcery.

7. Idolaters: They worship anyone or anything other than the one true God. They worship the idol of the anti-Christ during the Tribulation Period.

8. Liars: They deceive people by distorting the truth to lead people away from Jesus.

My wife, Glynis, loves to watch home renovation shows on television. A host takes a rundown house and turns it into a showplace. The owners put their trust in the contractor to remove a wall, change the cabinetry, renovate the kitchen and bathrooms, and paint everything a different color. This dilapidated home becomes a dream home. The highlight of the show is when the homeowners see their renovated home for the first time.

What will be your reaction when you step into your eternal home for the first time? Will your jaw hit the floor, stunned at the magnificent eternal Holy City?

When you think about your new eternal home through earthly eyes, you can't conceive of the beauty of Heaven. But if you dare look at your eternal home through spiritual eyes, Heaven can come into focus.

As the homeowner puts his and her trust in their contractor, you must put your trust in Jesus, your eternal contractor, who is building your eternal dream home right now (John 14:1-3).
He has promised you this home will be like nothing you have ever known. In this new home, the things in this world have passed away. Those things that cause sorrow, sufferings, tears, and temptations to God's children are dead. When God's people enter their home in Heaven, they will be at rest, living the peace and joy in the very presence of God Himself. What could be better?

Peter Baldwin Panagore, author of Heaven Is Beautiful, tells how he died on the side of a mountain in Canada. He says of his death experience: "That night on the mountain I learned that I had a new Home, which was my old Home, my first Home, my only Home, my real Home, and that Home is the one and only deep desire of my heart... My Home is heaven. It's your Home too."

Peter is right. Heaven is home. It's his home, my home, and every believer's home. But is it your home?

7 Points of Review

1. Your most valued possession will never stay new in this world. It's going to get old and die, including you. But everything you have in Heaven will never get old or die. You will live forever and everything you have will be yours forever.

2. When John saw a New Heaven and a New Earth, he saw "new" in quality. Before Adam and Eve sinned, the Earth was pristine and perfect. It was sinless and sacred. This is the New Earth you will inherit.

3. The Holy City, the New Jerusalem, is an actual city. It is not a state of mind, nor a figment of your imagination. Jesus is building this city right now in Heaven. It will reside in the New Heaven and the New Earth.

4. You have access to God today through the Holy Spirit and prayer. In eternal Heaven, you will have face-to-face access to God. You will talk with Him like you talk with your best friend.

5. Eternal Heaven is so great John describes it with the phrase, "no more." In Heaven, there's no more death, grief, crying, or pain. Anything that brings a tear to your eyes is nowhere in Heaven.

6. In this world, people view a Christian as weak and defeated, and they view the unsaved as strong and victorious. Don't lose sight. In eternity, there will be a reversal of fortune. The Christian is the victor, and the unsaved sinner is the loser.

7. We often say, "Home is where the heart is!" That truth will ring the loudest when you step into eternity forever.

1. What was the Earth like before Adam and Eve sinned in the Garden of Eden? How is it now? What will it be like in eternity?

   _____

   _____

   _____

   _____

2. Why is there a new arrangement of water on the New Earth?

   _____

   _____

   _____

   _____

3. What does it mean that God is, "Immanuel"?

   _____

   _____

   _____

   _____

4. John describes Heaven as the place of "no more." How do you describe Heaven?

_____

_____

_____

_____

5. Who are the victors?

_____

_____

_____

_____

Group Discussion Guide

MOTIVATION:

- Discuss your new stuff and how you try to keep it new as long as possible.

- Have you renovated, remodeled, or restored something back to its original condition? How did you feel when you completed the project?

EXAMINATION:

- Read Ecclesiastes 1:4, Psalm 78:69, and Psalm 104:5. Discuss why the Earth will last forever. Why doesn't God just start over with a brand-new Earth?

- Read 2 Peter 3:10-13. Discuss why you think the Earth needs to go through the refining and purifying process before it becomes the New Earth.

APPLICATION:

- Do not be defeated by the trials and tribulations of life on Earth. Thank God daily that you are victorious in Christ.

- Make Heaven your focus. Most people focus on their life on Earth. Their choices and decisions are based on their life here and now. I believe God wants you to focus on your eternal life in Heaven, and let that decide the choices and decisions you make on Earth. Choose today to live life focused on Heaven, not on Earth.

CHAPTER EIGHT: THE BEST PLACE YOU WILL EVER LIVE

The New Jerusalem appearing on the New Earth is everything the Garden of Eden was on the first Earth. This eternal city becomes a reality after the first Heaven and first Earth pass away, and the New Heaven and New Earth appear (Revelation 21:1). John has already mentioned the New Jerusalem coming down out of Heaven (v. 2); he now retraces his steps to give us the actual physical details of the eternal city. As we look at verses 9-14, notice the beauty and glory of God's hometown.

Revelation 21:9-14, "Then one of the seven angels, who had held the seven bowls filled with the seven last plagues, came and spoke with me: 'Come, I will show you the bride, the wife of the Lamb.' He then carried me away in the Spirit to a great and high mountain and showed me the holy city, Jerusalem, coming down out of heaven from God, arrayed with God's glory. Her radiance was like a precious stone, like a jasper stone, bright as crystal. The city had a massive high wall with 12 gates. Twelve angels were at the gates; on the gates, names were inscribed, the names of the 12 tribes of the sons of Israel. There were three gates on the east, three gates on the north, three gates on the south, and three gates on the west. The city wall had 12 foundations, and the 12 names of the Lamb's 12 apostles were on the foundations."

WHY IS THE CHURCH REFERRED TO AS THE "HOLY CITY"?

A city is known by its people, not by its building. The building, streets, lights, and businesses are there to aid the people. As John sees the "holy city," he sees the people of the city, who are the wife of the Lamb.

The angel who administered the seven bowls filled with the seven last plagues (Revelation 16) came and spoke to John. He showed John the bride, the wife of the Lamb, who is the church that returned with Jesus at His Second Coming (Revelation 19:11-16). Christ and His bride have been on the Earth for the millennial kingdom. They have finished their earthly honeymoon and are now ready to move into their eternal home and live in spiritual matrimony.

As I write this, I am reminded of my daughter's wedding. It's only been a week since Robbi and Mason were married. They gathered together with their family and friends, and we celebrated the physical and spiritual relationship God created. It was an honor to do the ceremony. I mentioned to Robbi and Mason, marriage on Earth is a picture of the eternal marriage we will have with Jesus in the New Jerusalem. God blesses us with the opportunity to experience on Earth what we are going to live in Heaven.

Jesus is building this city right now.

> John 14:1-4, "Your heart must not be troubled. Believe in God; believe also in Me. In My Father's house are many dwelling places; if not, I would have told you. I am going away to prepare a place for you. If I go away and prepare a place for you, I will come back and receive you to Myself, so that where I am you may be also. You know the way to where I am going."

Let me point out two biblical truths in this incredible passage. First, Jesus is preparing an actual place. When Jesus told the disciples that He was leaving to go prepare a place for them, He used language that describes an actual location. "Place" is the Greek word, "topos," from which we get our English word topography. It means the act of detailing the physical features of land on a map. In the New Testament, "topos" refers to an inhabited space. The context is an actual city or region. It also refers to a house or a room, as in John 14:2-3. "Dwelling" is the Greek word "mone." It's translated as habitat, lodging, or domicile. Again, the word is referring to an actual physical place. When Jesus said He was leaving to go prepare a dwelling place, He wasn't referring to a state of mind. He was referring to an actual physical place.

Second, Jesus uses "you" or "your" seven times in the passage. Why? He wants there to be no misunderstanding. This place is being built for you, His bride. You are the apple of Jesus' eye. He came for you, died for you, and resurrected for you. Everything Jesus is doing since arriving in Heaven after His ascension (Acts 1:9-14), has been to prepare for your arrival.

WHAT IS GOD'S GLORY?

As a pastor, one subject I love to teach and preach about is Heaven. I have preached several sermon series on the topic. The content in this book comes from those series. One question everyone asks, "What will eternal life be like in Heaven?" I always tell them, "It will be glorious!"

"God's glory," which John mentions in v. 11, is a divine dwelling of God's presence. The Jewish Rabbis coined the term "Shekinah Glory" to describe this dwelling of God. Moses saw the glory of God on Mt. Horeb in the burning bush (Exodus 3:1-17), and again when He asked to see the LORD's glory, and the LORD allowed Moses to see His back but not His face (Exodus 33:12-23).

This same glory was present with Israel in the wilderness. It was a cloud by day and a fire by night (Exodus 13:20-22). The glory of God surrounded Peter, James, and John at the Transfiguration (Matthew 17:1-13). The glory of God blinded Paul on the Damascus Road (Acts 9:1-8). John saw it in the Throne Room of God (Revelation 4). When we get to Heaven, we will see the glory of God. That glory is what John writes in Revelation 21.

WILL THE NEW EARTH HAVE MOUNTAINS?

John says the angel carried him to a high mountain (v. 10). Theologians say this is "a" mountain and not "the" mountain, which suggests more mountains. I believe it's possible.

Anyone who knows me knows I do not like cold climates. My wife asked me how I survived winters in Kentucky. I told her I knew nothing different. That changed when I arrived in Texas in 1983. The first December I wore shorts to the college cafeteria. I knew I wanted to live in Texas.

James Claborn, a prayer partner at my first pastorate, is an avid deer hunter. One Saturday night at our men's prayer group, James was talking about winter, being in the woods, and getting back to nature. Then he said to me, "Doesn't that sound good?" He knew I didn't like cold weather. I smiled and said, "If I'm in the woods, I'm lost!" James and the other men had a good laugh at my expense, and I laughed with them.

While I'm not a mountain man, I recognize how beautiful they are. I've been on church ski trips and looked across at the mountain peaks, marveling at what God had created.

Just as there are mountains on Earth, there will be mountains on the New Earth. These new mountains will be more majestic than any mountains we have now. Why do I say that? Because the mountains on the New Earth will be perfect. They are there to glorify God. In Luke 19:40, Jesus tells the Pharisees at His triumphal entry if the disciples didn't praise Him, the rocks would cry out. On the New Earth, maybe the mountains will cry out in praise to God.

HOW DOES JOHN DESCRIBE THE NEW JERUSALEM?

John does not shy away from describing the New Jerusalem as opulent. This city is extravagant. I believe this city is a crystal city, so the glory of God can shine throughout the city. There are no shadows in the city, because shadows are darkness, and we associate darkness with Satan, sin, and evil. Those things are not in eternal Heaven. As John says, the city is a clear crystal jasper stone.

There are two amazing facts regarding the Holy City: First, God dwelling in the city makes it the very center of the universe. Since Heaven, where God lives now, is the center of the universe, then the New Jerusalem, where God will live, is the new center of the universe. Second, the entire city is a precious jewel. Here's the good news, ladies. You won't have to worry about buying priceless jewelry in eternal Heaven. It will surround you. No need for a sapphire necklace, or an emerald bracelet, or a diamond ring. Every precious stone will surround you.

J. Vernon McGee said, "The New Jerusalem is a diamond in the gold mounting. This city is the engagement ring of the bride; in fact, it is the wedding ring. It is the symbol of the betrothal and wedding of the church to Christ."

WHAT'S THE PURPOSE OF ANGELS IN THE NEW JERUSALEM?

Cities in the Bible had gates for protection. The city officials stationed sentries to guard the gates. They checked everyone entering and exiting the city. In the New Jerusalem, God stations twelve angels at each of the twelve gates. These angels are not gatekeepers or sentries. They are not there for protection. Sin, war, and wickedness are non-existent in Heaven.

The angels magnify the city. They live in God's presence. His glory is reflected on everything around Him, including angels, especially the angels at the gates of the New Jerusalem.

Imagine you are exiting the southern gates of the New Jerusalem for a day of pleasure in a tropical paradise. Or, you are exiting the northern gates into a winter wonderland. As you exit, you look up at the angel stationed at his gate, and your eyes catch his eyes, and you just give each other a slight nod in passing. The kind you give when you pass someone on the street. But this nod is different, because it's one of fellowship. You're not passing a stranger on the street, you're passing an angel at his post, who is adding to the majesty of Heaven.

WHO ARE THE TWENTY-FOUR ELDERS?

It is my belief, and others with me, that the twenty-four elders are the twelve sons of Israel (Old Testament) and the twelve disciples of Jesus (New Testament). They worship Jesus by falling on their knees and removing their crowns, placing them before the throne.

> Revelation 4:4, 9-11, "Around that throne were 24 thrones, and on the thrones sat 24 elders dressed in white clothes, with gold crowns on their heads... Whenever the living creatures give glory, honor, and thanks to the One seated on the throne, the One who lives forever and ever, the 24 elders fall down before the One seated on the throne, worship the One who lives forever and ever, cast their crowns before the throne, and say: 'Our Lord and God, You are worthy to receive glory and honor and power, because You have created all things, and because of Your will they exist and were created.'"

The connection between the twelve sons of Israel and the twelve disciples of Jesus shows continuity between the Old Testament and the New Testament. The Old Testament predicts Jesus' coming, and the New Testament testifies to Jesus' coming.

Who are the sons of the twelve tribes of Israel whose names are engraved on the gates of the New Jerusalem?

The Twelve Sons of the Twelve Tribes of Israel

Reuben
Simeon
Judah
Dan
Naphtali
Gad
Asher
Issachar
Zebulun

Benjamin
Ephraim
Manasseh

When the tribes entered the Promised Land, Levi's descendants (Jacob's third son) did not inherit a territory for themselves (Joshua 13:14). Instead, they became priests of Israel, and built several cities scattered throughout the Promised Land. Joseph's tribe was divided between his two sons, Ephraim and Manasseh, giving Joseph a double portion. With all that Joseph went through in his life, hated by his brothers, sold into slavery, harassed by Potiphar's wife, falsely accused, thrown into prison, abandoned and forgotten, Joseph's faith never wavered. In fact, Joseph's faith grew stronger because of those experiences. As a result, Joseph's faithfulness to God saved his family from famine (Genesis 47:11-12). God rewarded Joseph by making Ephraim and Manasseh part of the twelve tribes.

Who are the twelve disciples whose names are engraved on the twelve foundations of the New Jerusalem?

The Twelve Disciples

Peter
John
James
Andrew
Philip
Thomas
Bartholomew
Matthew
James, the son of Alphaeus
Simon, the Zealot
Judas, the son of James
Matthias

I do not include the name of Judas Iscariot on the list. It is my opinion Judas Iscariot was not a true disciple of Jesus. Based on what Jesus said about Judas, along with the disciples, I believe he was not saved and has no inheritance of Heaven. I hope I am wrong. I want to see Judas in Heaven, but I don't think I will.

In closing, let me share a story of how glorious Heaven will be:

A widely respected man known as "Uncle Johnson" died in Michigan at the incredible age of 120. Perhaps his advanced years could be credited in part to the cheerful outlook that characterized his life. One day, while at work in his garden, he was singing songs of praise to God. His pastor, who was passing by, looked over the fence and called, "Uncle Johnson, you seem very happy today." "Yes, I was just thinking," said the old man. "Thinking about what?" questioned his pastor. "Oh, I was just thinking that if the crumbs of joy that fall from the Master's table in this world are so good, what will the great loaf in glory be like?"

You may have formed a mental picture of Heaven based on the Bible and the Book of Revelation. But whatever picture you have, eternal Heaven is beyond your wildest imagination. You will be in awe of God, as you see believers and angels worshipping at the throne of God. As you fall at Jesus' feet in worship, you will be speechless. It will be an indescribable scene to see Jesus in His glory.

7 Points of Review

1. In Heaven, we see the Shekinah Glory of God in the presence of both the Father and the Son. This glory is what John writes in Revelation 21.

2. The New Jerusalem is the place Jesus has gone to prepare (John 14:2). The words "you" or "your" are mentioned seven times. So, there will be no misunderstanding. Jesus is building this place for you, His bride, the church.

3. It's my belief that every form of nature we have on this Earth, we will have on the New Heaven, New Earth, and New Jerusalem, but in its purest form. We will have the best God created for our pleasure for eternity.

4. John describes the New Jerusalem as extravagant. Everywhere you look, you see precious jewels. I don't believe a shadow exists in the city, because shadows are darkness, and we associate darkness with Satan, sin, and evil in the Bible.

5. Two fantastic facts about the New Jerusalem: 1). It is the new center of the universe because God lives in the city. 2). Jesus builds the entire city as a precious jewel.

6. The angels stationed at the twelve gates are not there to protect the city. They are there to show the glory of God.

7. The connection between the twelve sons of Israel and the twelve disciples brings continuity between the Old Testament and the New Testament. The Old Testament predicts Jesus' coming and the New Testament testifies to Jesus' coming.

Big Questions

1. What is the "Shekinah Glory" of God?

    _____

    _____

    _____

    _____

2. In Revelation 21:9-10, why is the church referred to as the "holy city, Jerusalem"?

    _____

    _____

    _____

    _____

3. Do you believe that every form of nature we have on present Earth, we will have on the New Earth, but in its purest form? Why or why not?

    _____

    _____

    _____

    _____

4. What is the purpose of angels in the New Jerusalem?

_____

_____

_____

_____

5. In eternity, who are the twelve sons of Israel and the twelve disciples?

_____

_____

_____

_____

Group Discussion Guide

MOTIVATION:

- Ask the group to share a time when they heard God speak to them. How did it change their life?

- As a group, discuss your favorite city to visit, and share why you enjoy the city.

EXAMINATION:

- Read Revelation 21:9-14. In the passage, the "holy city" is personified as the bride. Why does God do this?

- Focus your time on The New Jerusalem. Discuss God's "Shekinah Glory" in the city, how John describes the city, and the purpose of angels in the city.

APPLICATION:

- What are you doing today to make sure God's glory is present in your life?

- If you're like most Christians, when you pray, you pray to the Father and the Son, but leave out the Holy Spirit. Yet the Holy Spirit is God's presence with us every day. This week, practice praying to the Holy Spirit. Mention Him by name. Take your requests to Him.

CHAPTER NINE:
THE JEWEL OF
HEAVEN

The real thing is best. Imitations are cheap and they never measure up. The genuine article is always better. For example, would you like to own a name-brand suit tailored from Italy, or own a second-rate suit from the local department store? Now, I didn't ask which suit you could afford, I just asked which suit you prefer to wear. You and I cannot afford the hand-cut suit from Italy, but it doesn't change the fact that it's a better suit.

In Revelation 21:15, John begins the physical description of the New Jerusalem. You need to know that it's an actual city. In fact, John calls it a "city" fifteen times in Revelation 21-22. The language in these two chapters is crystal clear. This is the best city ever built. There is an actual wall made of jasper, actual gates made of pearls, an actual street made of gold, and actual dwelling places. The holy, eternal city is one hundred percent real.

> Revelation 21:15-23, "The one who spoke with me had a gold measuring rod to measure the city, its gates, and its wall. The city is laid out in a square; its length and width are the same. He measured the city with the rod at 12,000 stadia. Its length, width, and height are equal. Then he measured its wall, 144 cubits, according to human measurement, which the angel

used. The building material of its wall was jasper, and the city was pure gold like clear glass.

The foundations of the city wall are adorned with every kind of precious stone:

the first foundation jasper,

the second sapphire,

the third chalcedony,

the fourth emerald,

the fifth sardonyx,

the sixth carnelian,

the seventh chrysolite,

the eighth beryl,

the ninth topaz,

the tenth chrysoprase,

the eleventh jacinth,

the twelfth amethyst.

The 12 gates are 12 pearls; each individual gate was made of a single pearl. The broad street of the city was pure gold, like transparent glass. I did not see a sanctuary in it, because the Lord God the Almighty and the Lamb are its sanctuary. The city does not need the sun or the moon to shine on it, because God's glory illuminates it, and its lamp is the Lamb."

HOW BIG IS THE CITY?

John measured the temple of God in Jerusalem (Revelation 11), now he's invited to witness the angel measuring the New Jerusalem. Notice how perfectly Jesus builds the city. There's no chip or crack in it. All four sides of the city are identical in length and width. Many believe the city is a cube, while others say it's a pyramid. Either way, it's built to perfection.

The city's measurements show this to be the largest city ever constructed. The wall is 216 feet thick (others say 216 feet high). Maybe it's both. The length, width, and height of the city is 12,000 stadia. One stadia is 600 feet, which correlates to 1,400 miles long, wide, and high. To understand how enormous this city is, it would cover the midwestern part of the United States, running from the western edge of the Appalachian Mountains to the eastern edge of the Rocky Mountains, and from the border of Canada to the state line of Texas. At 1,400 miles, it produces two million square miles of living surface. So that you can understand how big that is, New York City is 305 square miles. Many theologians believe the holy city has multiple levels. If so, how many people could live in this city? Millions, possibly a billion?

A few Bible scholars believe the measurements are symbolic. I see no reason to take these measurements figuratively. John is quick to point out that these are human measurements (v. 17). When we understand Jesus created the Heavens and Earth, building this holy city, even of this gigantic size, is a small building project for Him.

The size is not the only impressive thing about the city. The beauty and wealth are also impressive.

HOW WEALTHY IS THE CITY?

This is the most extravagant city ever built, and it's built for the bride of Christ. It is our reward for accepting Jesus' invitation to salvation. As we live in this eternal holy city, every precious gem stone known to man, and maybe a few unknown, surrounds us. The appearance and wealth of the city are beautiful. There is nothing in our finite minds that can help us understand the beauty of this city. When I think about a crystal city, I picture the Crystal Cathedral in Garden Grove, California. The tower over the entrance looks as if it rises out of the ground. The main building is reflective glass, including the roof. There are sculptures throughout the campus marking stories in the Bible, from Jesus walking on water, to the woman caught in adultery, and much more.

This beautiful church sold for $57.5 million in 2011. After a two-year, $72.3-million renovation, it now belongs to the Roman Catholic Diocese of Orange County, California. The New Jerusalem is never sold and is never renovated. It is perfect from the beginning and will be perfect for eternity.

WHAT IS THE BUILDING MATERIAL OF THE CITY?

John says the building materials of the city are precious gem stones. These stones are not just for beauty, but also for durability. They build walls on Earth for protection. In the holy city, Jesus built this wall for beauty. The wall of the city is jasper. I don't believe this jasper is the same stone we know on Earth; jasper stones we have on Earth are red. But John is describing a jasper stone that is crystal. I believe it's possible John is describing a diamond. Can you imagine the wall of the holy city being one diamond extending length, width, and height as far as the eye can see? John describes the city as pure gold, like glass. Maybe this diamond wall has a gold tint to it. Whether or not it does, it's beautiful to behold.

The city has twelve foundations. On Earth, foundations are underground, but not in the eternal city. These foundations are too beautiful to keep hidden.

The foundations of the city wall are precious stone:

the first foundation jasper (a reddish color),

the second sapphire (blue),

the third chalcedony (sky blue with streaks of other colors in it), the fourth emerald (bright green),

the fifth sardonyx (a red stone with streaks of white),

the sixth carnelian (a fiery red stone),

the seventh chrysolite (yellow and gold color),

the eighth beryl (a sea green color),

the ninth topaz (a brownish gold stone),

the tenth chrysoprase (a blue-green stone),

the eleventh jacinth (a violet-purple stone),

the twelfth amethyst (a purple stone).

I believe it's possible the holy city could have twelve separate levels, with each level divided by a foundation. This is just a guess, but if I'm right, imagine a diamond crystal city with gemstone foundations constructed throughout it.

As the wall of the city is for beauty, not protection, the same goes for the gates. Night doesn't exist in the city, so these gates are never closed.

While John addresses only the golden main street, I believe it's possible there are other streets in the city, but only the main street is transparent gold. I believe this main street could resemble a spiral staircase, extending from the southern gates of the city to the eastern and western gates, ending at the northern gates. This is only speculation, but it makes sense to me.

WHY DOESN'T THE CITY HAVE A CHURCH, TEMPLE, OR SANCTUARY?

The eternal city doesn't have a church, temple or sanctuary because it doesn't need one. The glory of God fills the city. God surrounded Peter, James, and John at the Transfiguration (Matthew 17), and He will surround you and me in the holy city.

What will we do in Heaven? As I've mentioned, I believe we will worship God, but not in a worship service as we do now. There's no need to go to a meeting place to have a church service. We are the church and God's presence surrounds us. Every moment of Heaven will be the purest worship we ever experience.

Someone once asked me, "Will there be arts, entertainment, and sports in Heaven?" "Yes!" I believe we will have the things that entertain us on Earth, but in their purest form. Every craft fair, movie, opera, play, or sporting event will exist to bring honor, glory, and worship to God. You will play and perform to the glory of God.

IN THE CITY, WILL WE HAVE PERSONAL ACCESS TO GOD?

The whole reason God comes to live with us in the holy city is to be with us. He is going to mix and mingle with His children. I believe we will see God walking in the city. Imagine having lunch with Jesus, or better yet, being invited to dine at God's supper table. Could you invite Jesus to your home for dinner? In Revelation 3:20, "Jesus said, 'Listen! I stand at the door and knock. If anyone hears my voice and opens the door, I will come in to him and have dinner with him, and he with me.'"

Is it possible I could pass God on the street and He would say to me, "Have a blessed day, Neale." "Thank you, God, I know I will."

In the Bible, the Jews believed that if they saw God's face, they would die. In the holy city, God is holy, and so are you. Because of that, I believe you and I will see God and have access to Him. This is the reason He comes to live with us.

7 Points of Review

1. Revelation 21-22 refers to the New Jerusalem as an actual city fifteen times. The city is cube shaped spanning 1,400 miles in length, width, and height. The living surface of the city is two million square miles.

2. Jesus perfectly constructed the city. There is nothing out of place. There are no chips, cracks, or cover-ups. It will never have to be renovated. It is perfect for eternity.

3. The eternal city is the most extravagant city ever built. It's built of every precious jewel.

4. I believe it's possible the twelve foundations of the New Jerusalem divide the holy city into twelve different levels. If I'm right, imagine each beautiful foundation extending throughout the holy city.

5. John says the main street of the city is transparent gold, and extends throughout the city like a spiral staircase, from the southern gates to the eastern and western gates, ending at the northern gates.

6. In the New Jerusalem, there will be worship, but not in a worship service. We will live in God's presence and experience the purest form of worship imaginable.

7. Imagine passing God on the Street of Gold, and He asks you, "How are you doing?" and you respond, "Perfect!"

1. In Revelation 21-22, how many times is the New Jerusalem referred to as a city? Why do you believe John does that?

_____

_____

_____

_____

2. What are the physical dimensions of the city? Describe how impressive that is to you.

_____

_____

_____

_____

3. Foundations on Earth are underground. Why are the twelve foundations of the New Jerusalem above ground? Do you agree or disagree the twelve foundations could divide the holy city into 1twelve different levels?

_____

_____

_____

_____

4. Does the golden street resembling a spiral staircase make sense to you? If not, what is your vision of the golden street?

_____

_____

_____

_____

5. Do you believe there will be arts, entertainment, and sports in Heaven? Why or why not?

_____

_____

_____

_____

Group Discussion Guide

MOTIVATION:

- Start the group time with a role play. Have one member play a person who believes Heaven is real, and another member play a person who believes Heaven is a state of mind. Debate the beliefs of both positions.

- Discuss the worship of eternal Heaven. Believers will worship in Heaven, but not in a worship service. What does the group think?

EXAMINATION:

- Read Matthew 6:19-20 and 19:21. Discuss the different things in Heaven and on Earth. Dig deep, think hard, and give several examples.

- Read over the physical description of the New Jerusalem in Revelation 21:15-23. Imagine the beauty and opulence of eternal Heaven. Now, imagine stepping into your eternal home for the first time. Describe your feelings and emotions.

APPLICATION:

- Jesus took His place on the cross so you could take your place in Heaven. What are you doing to ensure you have reserved your place in Heaven?

- What do you need to change right now to prepare for your eternal life with God in Heaven? Make the change. Don't wait for another day!

CHAPTER TEN: THE NATIONS OF HEAVEN

I have traveled little outside the United States. I've been to Mexico several times and to Ukraine once, with a stopover in London.

What I've noticed as I've traveled are the different cultures, and how they affect the way people dress, the food they eat, and their music. I live in Texas, and I don't need to travel far to dive deep into the Hispanic culture. I love Mexican food—fajitas, enchiladas, quesadillas, tacos, burritos, rice, beans, pico de gallo, and sopapillas. You name it; I like it. Well, almost everything—no guacamole!

A church I pastored traveled to Ukraine. It was my first visit to Europe. We flew into Kiev and then took an eight-hour overnight train to the Donetsk region in eastern Ukraine. The train whistle reminded me of the World War II movies I watched with my dad. The Ukrainian culture differed from our American culture. The people dressed differently, acted differently, talked differently, and we, Americans, stuck out like a sore thumb. Everyone knew the Americans were in town. People wanted to get their pictures taken with us. For a week, we immersed ourselves in their culture.

On our return trip to the United States, we had a two-day layover in London. England is a country with a long and rich history. We spent a full day sightseeing, going to the different historical landmarks, riding the double-decker buses and the Tube (the subway train), eating fish-n-chips, shopping for Union Jack sweatshirts (it's cold in July). We enjoyed getting to know the people of London—bus drivers, servers, hotel personnel. It was enlightening and educational!

What's my point? John mentions the nations will bring their worship into the holy city.

> Revelation 21:24-27, "The nations will walk in its light, and the kings of the earth will bring their glory into it. Each day its gates will never close because it will never be night there. They will bring the glory and honor of the nations into it. Nothing profane will ever enter it: no one who does what is vile or false, but only those written in the Lamb's book of life."

There's a consistent picture from the Old Testament prophets of a future king ruling from Jerusalem, bringing justice to the nations of the world.

> Isaiah 42:1, "This is My Servant; I strengthen Him, this is My Chosen One; I delight in Him. I have put My Spirit on Him; He will bring justice to the nations."

It's not surprising that the last verses of Revelation 21 give us the nations of the New Earth. Isaiah's vision is fulfilled in the New Heaven, New Earth, and New Jerusalem.

These verses are challenging to interpret, but I believe they are easy to understand. They are not teaching that everyone will live in Heaven. Revelation 20-22 is crystal clear, the wicked are cast into the Lake of Fire for eternity, and eternal Heaven is for saved believers in Jesus.

The "nations" and their "kings" are believers from the nations who live on the New Earth, while the Bride of Christ, the church, live in the New Jerusalem.

WHO ARE THE NATIONS AND THEIR KINGS?

I believe they are part of the "victors" mentioned in Revelation 21:7. While they do not inherit the New Jerusalem, they believe Jesus is the Messiah. They are from the earthly nations that come out of the Tribulation Period. They are believers because nothing profane enters the city, and no one who does what is vile or false, only those whose names appear in the Lamb's book of life.

Israel is among these nations. The Bible states that Israel has a forever future, even in the New Heaven and New Earth.

> Isaiah 66:22, "For just as the new heavens and the new earth, which I will make, will endure before Me,"—the Lord's declaration— "so will your offspring and your name endure."

> Ezekiel 39:25, "So this is what the Lord God says: Now I will restore the fortunes of Jacob and have compassion on the whole house of Israel, and I will be jealous for My holy name."

> Zephaniah 3:20, "At that time I will bring you back, yes, at the time I will gather you. I will give you fame and praise among all the peoples of the earth, when I restore your fortunes before your eyes. Yahweh has spoken."

WHAT DO THE NATIONS BRING INTO THE NEW JERUSALEM?

These nations do not live in the New Jerusalem, but they have access to it. They bring their glory, honor, praise, and worship to Jesus.

As they arrive to worship, the gates of the holy city are open. They can enter and exit just like the inhabitants of the city. Every day in the eternal city is a day of holiness.

It is my belief these nations are the same nations who populate the world from the past, present, and future. There will be Christians in every nation. Look what John writes:

> Revelation 5:9-10, "And they sang a new song: You are worthy to take the scroll and to open its seals; because You were slaughtered, and You redeemed people for God by Your blood from every tribe and language and people and nation. You made them a kingdom and priests to our God, and they will reign on the earth."

God's plan for eternity is for people to live on the New Earth, and they come into the New Jerusalem to praise and worship the KING OF KINGS. This reminds me of Jesus' first coming, when the Kings of the East came to worship the Messiah in Bethlehem. Many believe the kings were from Persia, which today is modern day Iran. The picture is the same, earthly kings coming to Jesus' home to pay tribute to Him. Christianity is the only true world-wide religion on Earth today, and it will continue to be so in eternity.

IS IT POSSIBLE THERE COULD BE DIFFERENT CULTURES IN THE NEW JERUSALEM?

It's more than possible, John says it's a certainty. These nations and their kings will not only bring their worship into the holy city, they also bring their cleansed, redeemed, and purified cultures.

Just as Chicago has Polish Downtown, Los Angeles has Thai Town, and New York City has Chinatown, the New Jerusalem will have the cleansed, purified, and redeemed cultures of Argentina, Austria, Ethiopia, Germany, Iran, Japan, Morocco, Peru, Russia, Spain, Vietnam, Zimbabwe, and even the Native American Indians, the Aborigines of Australia, and the Eskimos of Canada. Every nation from the start of creation will be present in the holy city. Cultures like the ancient Aztecs, Babylonians, Mayans, Persians, and Vikings, just to name a few. How do I know this? I believe two Old Testaments prophets predict it:

> Daniel 7:14, "He was given authority to rule, and glory, and a kingdom; so that those of every people, nation, and language should serve Him. His dominion is an everlasting dominion that will not pass away, and His kingdom is one that will not be destroyed."

I believe the key word in the verse is "every," which I interpret to be all people, nations, and languages, past, present, and future.

> Isaiah 60:11, "Your gates will always be open; they will never be shut day or night so that the wealth of the nations may be brought into you, with their kings being led in procession."

When Isaiah says "the wealth of nations may be brought into you," I believe it's a sign that the New Jerusalem will be an international city.

My Christmas present to Glynis in 2019 was tickets to the Opera House in Dallas for a Chinese cultural experience called "Shen Yun." It was a two-hour dance experience tracing the different dance styles through the history of the Chinese culture. Is it possible in the New Jerusalem, similar performances could be part of the entertainment you and I will experience? Yes! I believe it's more than possible.

As I read Scripture, I believe there will be many nations and their different cultures on the New Earth, and the kings of those redeemed nations will bring their people into the New Jerusalem to worship Jesus.

WHO ARE THOSE WHOSE NAMES ARE WRITTEN IN THE LAMB'S BOOK OF LIFE?

They are the saved believers who have accepted Jesus' invitation to eternal life. They are the redeemed of God.

John records who will be there, but he records three times who will not be there (Revelation 21:8, 27; 22:15). The eternal holy city is for the professed, not for the profane.

Who will be there? God and His redeemed humanity–v. 3; the Alpha and Omega–v. 6; victors/overcomers–v. 7; the bride–v. 10; angels–v. 12;

Israel's sons–v. 12; Jesus' disciples–v. 14; the Lamb–v. 23; redeemed nations and their kings–v. 24; and those whose name God wrote in the Lamb's book of life–v. 27.

What will be there? Great wealth, beauty, and opulence. God's glory and His throne will be there.

What will not be there? No tears, no death, no grief, no crying, and no pain–v. 4; no sanctuary–v. 22; no sun or moon–v. 23; and no night–v. 25.

Who will not be there? Cowards, unbelievers, the vile, murderers, the sexually immoral, sorcerers, idolaters, and liars–v. 8; the profane, the vile, the false–v. 27; the dogs, the sorcerers, the sexually immoral, the murderers, the idolaters, and everyone who lies–22:15.

Let me close this chapter by saying you don't need to wonder if you're going to Heaven. You don't need to cross your fingers and hope you get there. You can know your name is written in the Lamb's book of life. God is still taking reservation for Heaven. Trust Him today and secure your home in Heaven. Turn to A-B-C of Salvation in the back of the book, and walk your way into eternal life.

1. Just as the present Earth has an international flavor, with many cultures, the New Heaven, the New Earth, and the New Jerusalem also have the same international flavor.

2. The nations who enter the holy city are the saved and redeemed believers in Jesus.

3. Revelation 20-22 is very clear, unsaved sinners are thrown into the Lake of Fire (see Revelation 20:7-10; 21:8; 22:15).

4. The Magi coming to worship the newborn Messiah in Bethlehem is an example of the nations of the Earth and their kings coming to worship Jesus in the New Jerusalem.

5. In the New Jerusalem, it's possible that every culture, past, present, and future, will be present for eternity.

6. In the New Jerusalem, there will be great joy because of the wealth and beauty of the city.

7. There is no sadness in New Jerusalem. Death, grief, crying, and pain do not exist in eternal Heaven.

1. Who are the nations and their kings that enter the city?

   _____

   _____

   _____

   _____

2. Why is Christianity the only true worldwide religion?

   _____

   _____

   _____

   _____

3. Do you think there could be international cultures in the New Jerusalem? Why or why not?

   _____

   _____

   _____

   _____

4. Who has access to the New Jerusalem?

_____

_____

_____

_____

5. Who does NOT have access to the city?

_____

_____

_____

_____

Group Discussion Guide

MOTIVATION:

- Discuss as a group the different cultures you have encountered as you've traveled abroad.

- What did you like about the culture? What didn't you like about the culture?

EXAMINATION:

- Read Revelation 21:1-23. Discuss who will be in Heaven. Who will not be in Heaven? What will be in Heaven? What will not be in Heaven?

- Read Revelation 21:24-27. Discuss the international flavor in Heaven. Do you think multi-cultural worship could be present in eternal Heaven? Using your imagination, or experience, how is worship different from culture to culture? How is it the same?

APPLICATION:

- Choose two or three cultures and study how they worship God. Talk to people from those countries, or to missionaries who have served there. Use your own experiences from mission trips you've taken.

- Heaven will be multi-cultural and international. Connect with a person from another culture and begin a Bible study.

CHAPTER ELEVEN: THE GARDEN OF EDEN, RESTORED

As I write this chapter, I'm attending a Southern Gospel concert hosted at the church I pastor. It's January and outside it's raining and cold, but the weather has not affected the attendance. There is a joyous spirit in the church tonight. Most attending the concert are in the twilight of their life. The younger generations refer to them as senior adults.

As I attend the concert, I am struck because many Southern Gospel songs are about Heaven and living with Jesus. Heaven is referred to as "A City Called Glory," and "Sweet Beulah Land." There are songs entitled, "A Walk Around Heaven" and "The First Morning in Heaven."

As John continues his description of Heaven's holy city, I can't help but imagine the day you and I will step into this city for the first time. It will be our home and have everything we need for life in eternity. It will have every believing Christian that has ever lived. But most importantly, it will have Jesus, the Lamb. This city is paradise, the Garden of Eden, restored (Revelation 2:7).

> Revelation 22:1-5, "Then he showed me the river of living water, sparkling like crystal, flowing from the throne of God and of the Lamb down the middle of the broad street of the city. The tree of life was on both sides of the river, bearing 12 kinds of

fruit, producing its fruit every month. The leaves of the tree are for healing the nations, and there will no longer be any curse. The throne of God and of the Lamb will be in the city, and His slaves will serve Him. They will see His face, and His name will be on their foreheads. Night will no longer exist, and people will not need lamplight or sunlight, because the Lord God will give them light. And they will reign forever and ever."

As we move into Revelation 22, we discover the Bible ends where it begins. Time began in a garden paradise, and time ends in a city paradise. Genesis 2-3, record paradise lost and Revelation 21-22, record paradise restored. Notice the consequences of sin introduced in Genesis that are resolved in Revelation:

G: Humanity rebels against God.
R: All rebellion has ceased.

G: The serpent separates Adam and Eve from God.
R: God throws the serpent into the Lake of Fire.

G: The curse of sin bars man from paradise.
R: The curse is reversed, and God's people live with Him in paradise.

G: Pain and suffering enter the world.
R: Pain and suffering no longer exist.

G: God bars Man from the Tree of Life.
R: God's people eat fruit from the Tree of Life.

In Revelation 22:1-2, John gives us three settings of nature that appeared in the Garden of Eden, and will also appear in the New Jerusalem:

WHAT IS THE RIVER OF LIVING WATER?

Just as water is important to present Earth, it's also important to the New Earth. Human beings need water for life on Earth, and that doesn't change in eternity. Even in Heaven, eternal life is still life, and all life needs water to survive.

The River of Life flowing from God's throne means God supplies the pure, thirst-quenching life in Heaven. In John 10:10, Jesus says, "I have come that they may have life, and have it abundantly." The New Jerusalem is the very definition of the "abundant life."

This river flows down the holy city's street of gold. The exact architecture of the river and the street of gold is unclear. Does the river divide the street, or does the street divide the river? It's not possible to know for sure. Either way, the River of Living Water feeds into the Tree of Life.

Could there be smaller streams flowing off the main river to other parts of the city? I believe it's possible. In our world today, major rivers feed water into smaller streams that fill the Earth's landscape. I have waded into those streams, scooped up water in my hand for a refreshing drink. Imagine families having a picnic on the banks of the great river, laughing and playing, sweeping their hands in the water, and looking into the crystal-clear water.

In the Garden of Eden, there was a great river that gave life and nourishment to the garden paradise (Genesis 2:10). Now there's another great river giving life to God's new paradise. The river takes me back to Jesus meeting the woman at the well.

> John 4:13-14, "Everyone who drinks from this water will get thirsty again. But whoever drinks from the water that I will give him will never get thirsty again—ever! In fact, the water I will give him will become a well of water springing up within him for eternal life."

I believe it's possible that Jesus was referring to the River of Living Water, as He talked with the woman at the well. It's possible these verses in John 4 will take on a whole new meaning in the New Jerusalem.

WHAT IS THE TREE OF LIFE?

Is it one massive tree with a split trunk and the river flowing through the middle of the tree? This makes sense to me, since the tree is on both sides of the river. Some believe the Tree of Life is not one tree, but an orchard of trees filling the landscape on both sides of the river. We can't be sure of the exact design, and it doesn't matter to speculate. What matters is the Tree of Life in the Garden of Eden (Genesis 2:9) is the same tree in the New Jerusalem.

The Tree of Life is the only vegetation mentioned in the eternal city, but don't assume it's the only vegetation. I don't believe it is. As I believe the River of Living Water flows throughout the city, into smaller streams, and maybe over beautiful waterfalls, I also believe there are other trees throughout the city. The main root of the Tree of Life may have roots in these trees.

John mentions that the Tree of Life produces twelve different fruits each month. But he does not mention how the tree produces the fruit. Some scholars believe the Tree of Life produces a different fruit each month. Other scholars believe the Tree of Life produces twelve different fruits every month. I'm good either way.

The prophet Ezekiel echoes this description of the Tree of Life and its yielded fruit.

> Ezekiel 47:12, "All kinds of trees providing food will grow along both banks of the river. Their leaves will not wither, and their fruit will not fail. Each month they will bear fresh fruit because the water comes from the sanctuary. Their fruit will be used for food and their leaves for medicine."

Both Ezekiel 47:12 and Revelation 22:2 reveal the third setting of nature in the New Jerusalem, the leaves on the Tree of Life. It seems they have medicinal purposes.

WHY DO THE LEAVES OF THE TREE HEAL THE NATIONS?

John says the leaves are healing for the nations. But wait a minute, I thought there's no sickness, disease, death, or pain in eternal Heaven? You are correct. So, what and who needs healing? For the answers, let me quote two passages from Randy Alcorn in his book *Heaven: A*

Comprehensive Guide to Everything the Bible Says About Our Eternal Home.

"Some people find it hard to understand why perfectly healthy people will need food, water, and health-giving vegetation on the New Earth. It appears that we will still have needs, but they will be met. The organic nature of edible fruit and medicinal leaves emphasizes the tie of mankind to Earth, suggesting that eternal life won't be as different from life in Eden as is often assumed."

"Why couldn't we tumble while climbing on the New Earth? Won't there be gravity? Adam and Eve couldn't die, but couldn't they skin their knees? God didn't originally create bodies without nerve endings, did he? Perhaps they could fall, do minor damage, and then heal quickly. We're told that on the New Earth there'll be no more death, crying, or pain (Revelation 21:4). But we're also told, 'The leaves of the tree are for the healing of the nations' (Revelation 22:2). No one will suffer or die on the New Earth, but this passage suggests that there might be minor damage to require healing."

As crazy as it may be to you and me, the New Earth is a place of healing. Christ healed every person brought to Him when He was on the Earth. Could His healing ministry be a pre-curser to what you and I will experience in Heaven?

DID GOD HAVE A REDEMPTIVE PLAN FOR THE WORLD FROM THE BEGINNING?

When God created Adam and Eve and placed them in the Garden of Eden, it started out sinless, Satan-less, and death-less. All that changed when the first couple made the dreadful decision to disobey God and eat from the forbidden tree (Genesis 2:17). When that happened, everything on God's perfect Earth changed. It was a dark day.

Ever since the Fall of Man in the Garden of Eden (Genesis 3), the Earth and humanity have been living under an awful curse. God gives us a promise to one day reverse the curse:

Genesis 3:15, "I will put hostility between you and the woman, and between your seed and her seed. He will strike your head, and you will strike his heel."

Theologians call this verse "protoevangelium," which means, "the first gospel" or "the first good news." This verse is part of a conversation between God and Satan after sin came into the world. From this conversation comes a ray of hope for the world. Let's break the verse down to see its meaning.

"I will put hostility between you and the woman." God speaks these words to the serpent, who is Satan. God is saying that He desires no relationship with Satan. The two are totally opposite in every way.

"And between your seed and her seed." The serpent's seed refers to Satan, and the woman's seed is Jesus (see Galatians 3:16). The hostility between Satan and Jesus continues today through the spiritual warfare between humanity and the forces of evil (Ephesians 6:12).

"He (Jesus) will strike your head." A fatal blow. Jesus' ultimate victory over Satan came at the Cross, when Jesus crushed Satan, his evil kingdom, and his influence over the souls of humanity. At the Cross, Jesus delivered a fatal blow to Satan. John records Satan's final defeat in Revelation 20:10.

"And you (Satan) will strike his heel." A non-fatal blow. Satan cannot kill Jesus. Satan had significant influence over those who crucified Jesus, but the Bible is crystal clear. Jesus did not die at the hand of Satan or those he influenced. No! Jesus died and rose again to save humanity from sin. Many scholars believe this non-fatal blow refers to the Messiah's suffering. Isaiah expands on this idea of the Suffering Servant.

> Isaiah 53:1-9, "Who has believed what we have heard? And who has the arm of the Lord been revealed to? He grew up before Him like a young plant and like a root out of dry ground. He had no form or splendor that we should look at Him, no appearance that we should desire Him. He was despised and rejected by men, a man of suffering who knew what sickness was. He was like one people turned away from; He was despised, and we didn't value Him. Yet He Himself bore our sicknesses, and He carried our pains; but we in turn regarded Him stricken, struck down by God, and afflicted. But He was

pierced because of our transgressions, crushed because of our iniquities; punishment for our peace was on Him, and we are healed by His wounds. We all went astray like sheep; we all have turned to our own way; and the Lord has punished Him for the iniquity of us all. He was oppressed and afflicted, yet He did not open His mouth. Like a lamb led to the slaughter and like a sheep silent before her shearers, He did not open His mouth. He was taken away because of oppression and judgment; and who considered His fate? For He was cut off from the land of the living; He was struck because of My people's rebellion. They made His grave with the wicked, and with a rich man at His death, although He had done no violence and had not spoken deceitfully."

Bible scholars believe God had a redemptive plan through His Son from the very beginning:

Romans 8:29, "For those He foreknew He also predestined to be conformed to the image of His Son, so that He would be the firstborn among many brothers."

Romans 9:23-24, "And what if He did this to make known the riches of His glory on objects of mercy that He prepared beforehand for glory—on us, the ones He also called, not only from the Jews but also from the Gentiles?"

Ephesians 1:4, "For He chose us in Him, before the foundation of the world, to be holy and blameless in His sight."

Genesis 3:15, written at the beginning of the Bible, long before Jesus' death on the cross, proves God directed every word of the Bible and directs every event in history. He has a sovereign plan for the world and it's accomplished to perfection.

What's the opposite of a curse? A blessing. God cursed humanity in the Garden, now He blesses them in Heaven. In Revelation 21-22, there are seven things that will be "no more" in Heaven: no sea, no death, no grief, no crying, no pain, no night, and now, no curse. Notice in Revelation 22:3-5 there are four great blessings of the curse reversed: His servants will serve Him. They will see His face. His name will be on their foreheads. They will reign forever and ever.

What makes Heaven so great? There is no hint of sin or its curse. It has been reversed. You and I are the beneficiaries of Jesus' death on the cross. Now comes the final greatest blessing of life in Heaven.

WHY ARE WE ABLE TO SEE GOD IN HEAVEN, BUT NOT NOW?

Today, you and I see with imperfect eyes through an imperfect body in an imperfect world. If you're like me, you either have corrective glasses or contacts. When we're resurrected to Heaven, our vision is corrected physically and spiritually. Things concealed to us in this world are revealed to us in the new world.

To see God face-to-face means you have gone through a radical transformation. It means you have become righteous and sinless, and this creates an indescribable joy within your soul that will never cease.

Just think about it! We will see the beauty and perfection of God daily as we live with Him forever. His name will be on our foreheads, as a sign of our loyalty and allegiance to Him, and as a sign of His ownership.

Many of us do not think twice about wearing the name of our favorite team splashed across our chest on a T-shirt, or the team logo embroidered on a cap we wear on our heads. We call it, "Team spirit!" The ultimate team spirit will be when we have God's name on our foreheads.

If we are going to see God, then we also talk to Him. Today we talk to God in our prayers, but in Eternal Heaven we will talk to God face to face. Can you imagine asking Him all the questions you've wanted answered?

John tells us in verse 5 that seeing God's face will mean that we will reign with Him forever. He has already mentioned in Revelation 21:23, the holy city does not need a sun or moon to shine on it, because the glory of God will illuminate the city. He gets specific when he says the Lamb of God (Jesus) is the lamp of the city. Now, John adds, the city never experiences night, and no one needs a lamplight or sunlight, or a flashlight.

God's children will fulfill on the New Earth what God assigned to Adam and Eve on the old Earth:

> Genesis 1:28, "Be fruitful, multiply, fill the earth, and subdue it. Rule the fish of the sea, the birds of the sky, and every creature that crawls on the earth."

David confirms God's command when he writes:

> Psalm 8:6, "You made him lord over the works of Your hands; You put everything under his feet."

It's obvious God has a future plan for the Earth. His plan involves a kingdom that will last forever. This kingdom John writes about in Revelation 22:1-5 is real. He saw it with his own eyes. He saw the glory of God, and he saw the saints serving and reigning with God.

You can see what John saw, and you can experience what John experienced. How? Accept Jesus' gift of eternal life. Because to be Heaven bound, you must be Heaven born.

7 Points of Review

1. Time begins in a garden paradise. Time ends in a city paradise. Genesis 3 records paradise lost. Revelation 22 records paradise restored.

2. In the Garden of Eden, there was a great river that gave life and nourishment to God's original paradise (Genesis 3). In the New Jerusalem, there's another great river flowing from God's throne that gives life and nourishment to God's permanent paradise.

3. The Tree of Life, present in the original garden, produced both physical and spiritual provisions. These same provisions are present with the Tree of Life in the New Jerusalem.

4. According to Randy Alcorn, in his book, *Heaven*, there may still be skinned knees and scraped elbows. While there's no death, there may be minor injuries, and the leaves of the Tree of Life speed up the healing process.

5. Protoevangelium (Genesis 3:15) shows that God has a redemptive plan for humanity from the start of creation. But it also shows that God directed every word of the Bible, and every event in history.

6. The Bible states God visited with Adam and Eve in the Garden of Eden. That means they saw Him face to face. Direct contact with God will be restored on the New Earth when God comes to live with His people.

7. God's children will fulfill on the New Earth what God assigned Adam and Eve on the old Earth. Genesis 1:28 says, "God blessed them, and God said to them, 'Be fruitful, multiply, fill the earth, and subdue it. Rule the fish of the sea, the birds of the sky, and every creature that crawls on the earth.'"

1. In the chapter, there are six themes introduced in Genesis 1-3 that are resolved in Revelation 20-22. What are those six themes?

_____

_____

_____

_____

2. What is the River of Life?

_____

_____

_____

_____

3. What is the Tree of Life?

_____

_____

_____

_____

4. What's the purpose of the leaves from the Tree of Life?

    _____

    _____

    _____

    _____

5. What is protoevangelium? Explain it in your own words:

    _____

    _____

    _____

    _____

MOTIVATION:

- Growing a vegetable garden or planting flowers to brighten up the landscape of your home takes a lot of work. Share with the group your success or failure at gardening.

- When Adam and Eve had dominion over the Garden of Eden, it was perfect, and they were perfect. Do you think they worked to keep the garden in perfect condition, or was it perfect on its own?

EXAMINATION:

- Eternal Heaven is the Garden of Eden restored. Using the six themes mentioned in this chapter, discuss the things lost in the Garden of Eden that are restored in the New Jerusalem. Why is the New Earth better than the Garden of Eden?

- Discuss the "River of living water, sparkling like crystal flowing from the throne of God," "The tree of life bearing 12 kinds of fruit, producing its fruit every month," and "The leaves of the tree are for the healing of the nations." In your interpretation of these verses, how are they connected?

APPLICATION:

- If you have never tried growing a garden, try it. Start small with just a few plants. Talk to a nursery owner. They can get you started off on the right foot.

- Research the healing properties of water, and the nutritional value of eating more fruit. Maybe choose a day of the week as your "Fruit Fasting Day." You'll be getting yourself ready for life in eternity.

CHAPTER TWELVE:
THE END IS
THE BEGINNING

When the entertainment industry started producing silent movies, the last frame of the film read, "The End." That let the audience know the movie was over. As we come to the last verses of John's Revelation, we come to "The End."

But wait a minute. If Heaven is eternal, how can it be, "The End"? That's a great question. I agree with you. Heaven is eternal and forever, but it's also the end. The end of death as we know it, the end of sin as we know it, and the end of time as we know it. While Heaven is the end of many things on Earth, it's the beginning of what we can only imagine. One day we won't have to imagine Heaven. We will live in it forever.

In Revelation 22:6-21, John and Jesus give us the Bible's Benediction. These verses are one complete thought, and it's God's last message to His children.

> Revelation 22:6-21, "Then he said to me, 'These words are faithful and true. And the Lord, the God of the spirits of the prophets, has sent His angel to show His servants what must quickly take place.'
>
> 'Look, I am coming quickly! Blessed is the one who keeps the prophetic words of this book.'

I, John, am the one who heard and saw these things. When I heard and saw them, I fell down to worship at the feet of the angel who had shown them to me. But he said to me, 'Don't do that! I am a fellow slave with you, your brothers the prophets, and those who keep the words of this book. Worship God.' He also said to me, 'Don't seal the prophetic words of this book, because the time is near. Let the unrighteous go on in unrighteousness; let the filthy go on being made filthy; let the righteous go on in righteousness; and let the holy go on being made holy.'

'Look! I am coming quickly, and My reward is with Me to repay each person according to what he has done. I am the Alpha and the Omega, the First and the Last, the Beginning and the End.'

Blessed are those who wash their robes, so that they may have the right to the tree of life and may enter the city by the gates. Outside are the dogs, the sorcerers, the sexually immoral, the murderers, the idolaters, and everyone who loves and practices lying.

I, Jesus, have sent My angel to attest these things to you for the churches. I am the Root and the Offspring of David, the Bright Morning Star.

Both the Spirit and the bride say, 'Come!' Anyone who hears should say, 'Come!' And the one who is thirsty should come. Whoever desires should take the living water as a gift.

I testify to everyone who hears the prophetic words of this book: If anyone adds to them, God will add to him the plagues that are written in this book. And if anyone takes away from the words of this prophetic book, God will take away his share of the tree of life and the holy city, written in this book.

He who testifies about these things says, 'Yes, I am coming quickly.'

Amen! Come, Lord Jesus!

The grace of the Lord Jesus be with all the saints. Amen."

WHY IS JOHN TOLD NOT TO SEAL THE PROPHETIC WORDS OF THE BOOK?

John is told to keep his book open, because the time is near.

Revelation 22:10, "He also said to me, 'Don't seal the prophetic words of this book, because the time is near.'"

In contrast, the prophet Daniel was told as he closed his book to seal up the words and keep them secret until the end.

> Daniel 8:26, "The vision of the evenings and the mornings that has been told is true. Now you must seal up the vision because it refers to many days in the future."
>
> Daniel 12:4, "But you, Daniel, keep these words secret and seal the book until the time of the end. Many will roam about, and knowledge will increase."
>
> Daniel 12:9, "He said, 'Go on your way, Daniel, for the words are secret and sealed until the time of the end.'"

What has happened in the 600 years from Daniel's prophecy to John's prophecy? The simple answer is, Jesus has happened. God has determined, now is the time to offer humanity God's salvation through Jesus' sacrifice on the Cross. It's time for humanity to hear the gospel, and hearing the gospel forces humanity to decide about Jesus. This decision about Jesus will determine one's eternal destination. John states, at Jesus' return, some will be unrighteous, doing filthy deeds, and some will be righteous, doing holy deeds (Revelation 22:11).

WHAT'S THE WARNING OF JESUS' RETURN?

Jesus coming quickly is a reference to both the Rapture and the Second Coming. The Rapture happens, "In the twinkling of an eye" (1 Corinthians 15:52). This is so quick, it's instant. While the Second Coming doesn't happen instantly, Christ's return is quick. According to Revelation 19:11-16, the world is in total darkness when John saw Heaven open and Jesus, along with His armies, burst into the world, riding white horses and wearing white robes. Jesus comes to conquer the nations that have denied Him as KING OF KINGS AND LORD OF LORDS. When Jesus comes, there's no time to repent.

Jesus' return is a time of judgment, to repay the unrighteous what they deserve. But Jesus' return is also a reward. Who is Jesus rewarding? The righteous and holy (Revelation 22:11), and the blessed, who have washed their robes (Revelation 22:14). Note the blessed wash their own robes. This must be a reference to humanity's choice to accept Jesus' invitation to salvation. You don't get into Heaven on your parent's or grandparent's salvation. The only way to Heaven is by accepting Jesus as your Savior.

What's the reward? They will eat of the Tree of Life and they will enter the New Jerusalem through the gates (Revelation 22:14).

When I imagine a tree and life, I imagine a tree leading to eternal life. That tree is the Cross of Christ's crucifixion. When the Romans adopted crucifixion from the Greeks and Carthaginians, it was a symbol of death. Perfected by the Romans, crucifixion inflicted pain, torture, and humiliation on its victims. Jesus took their symbol of death and turned it into a symbol of life. It's through Jesus' death on the Cross that you and I have eternal life.

WHAT DOES IT MEAN THAT JESUS IS THE ALPHA AND OMEGA, THE FIRST AND THE LAST, THE BEGINNING AND THE END, THE ROOT AND OFFSPRING OF DAVID, THE BRIGHT MORNING STAR?

These titles describe His eternal nature. The Alpha and Omega describe Jesus as the Word (John 1:1, 14). He is the first letter and the last letter, and all the letters in between. It was common among the Jewish rabbis to use the Alpha and Omega of the Hebrew alphabet to denote the whole thing. He is the author of creation (John 1:3), and He is the author of re-creation (John 14:1-3). He is the author and finisher of our faith (Hebrews 12:2).

Jesus is the First and the Last. He's on the first page of the Bible, and He is on the last page of the Bible, and all the pages in between. He's in the first book of the Bible and He is in the last book of the Bible, and all the books in between. He's in the first verse of Genesis, and He is in the last verse of Revelation. One could say that Jesus is the first testament of God (Old Testament), and He is the last testament of God (New Testament). Jesus says:

> Revelation 1:17-18, "Don't be afraid! I am the First and the Last, and the Living One. I was dead, but look—I am alive forever and ever, and I hold the keys of death and Hades."

This verse states two important details. First, Jesus is eternal (cf. Micah 5:2; Isaiah 9:6; John 1:1, 8:58). Second, Jesus is unique. Christianity stands against the other world religions, in the sense that our God is alive, and their gods are dead.

The third title Jesus gives: He is the Beginning and the End. Salvation begins and ends with Jesus. From justified sinners to the sanctified saints. Whatever He starts, He finishes. He was there at the beginning of time (Genesis 1:1), and He will be there at the end of time (Revelation 21:3).

Jesus is the Root and Offspring of David. This shows Jesus' connection with humanity and human history. Matthew 1:1-16 and Luke 3:23-38 trace Jesus' lineage through King David. Many of Jesus' ancestors were princes and prophets, but all were sinners.

This title shows Jesus' connection with the Jewish race. Jesus was born a Jew, raised a Jew, and died a Jew. In the divine scheme of God's plan, God decided the Jewish nation produces humanity's Redeemer. There is no use arguing this. It's a fact and it will not change.

As the Root and Offspring of David, Jesus shows the royal line of King David that points to Jesus as the KING OF KINGS and LORD OF LORDS. When Jesus establishes His eternal kingdom on Earth, King David will be there, sitting at the righthand of Jesus, leading the nation of Israel for eternity (Jeremiah 30:9; Ezekiel 37:24).

The last title Jesus gives: He is the Bright Morning Star. This is a metaphor meaning that Jesus outshines all other stars (gods). Jesus is the most holy and most powerful light in the universe. He refers to

Himself as the "Light of the World" in John 8:12 and 9:5. He is the Light because He is self-existent.

It's important to note that Satan is referred to as the "morning star," but only as a poor imitation of Jesus. I have often taught in Bible Studies Satan is a copycat of God. He's a God-wannabe. The whole reason God kicked him out of Heaven is because he tried to usurp God's authority. Many theologians believe Isaiah 14:12-15 is Satan's fall from Heaven. Isaiah 14:15 states that Satan will rest in Sheol, the deepest regions of the pit, no doubt a reference to his ultimate resting place in the Lake of Fire (Revelation 20:10).

Revelation 22:16 is the first mention of the church in the book since Revelation 3:22. The Greek word "attest" means to acknowledge. It means the same thing as our English words "authenticate" and "approve." Several Bible translations use the word "testify." God sent this angel to acknowledge, approve, attest, and authenticate the entire book of Revelation.

What do "these things" refer to? It is my belief that Jesus is referring to John's four visions in the book. God intended the four visions for the seven churches in Revelation 2-3. I listed the visions in the Introduction of the book.

WHO IS CALLED TO COME TO CHRIST?

John states the call to "Come" is an invitation to the world. "Anyone" and "Whoever" (v. 17) means everyone. Notice in 22:17, it's the Holy Spirit and the Bride (the New Testament believers) who call the world to come to Jesus. The Holy Spirit and the Bride work together to evangelize the world. The Bride witnesses to the lost, and the Holy Spirit convicts the lost (John 16:8). So, they join to call the world to Jesus. This verse may be one of the most evangelistic verses in the Bible.

It is our responsibility to invite others to Jesus. Only those who have heard the call and accepted the call can invite others to salvation. I remember the first person I witnessed to after I accepted Christ was a neighborhood friend. He and I are best friends. As kids, we played ball together, rode bikes together, and when we became teenagers, went on double-dates with our girlfriends together. It was a few years later I had the pleasure of seeing him baptized. I would not have witnessed to him if I didn't have Jesus in my own life. We share with others what is important to us. Jesus is important to me, and so I share Him with others.

There are two metaphors in verse 17. The "thirsty" are those who seek God. They thirst for the answer to life's purpose. For you and me, evangelism is to make people thirsty for Jesus. We should live in a way that the world sees Jesus in our hearts, and they want Him in their hearts. That's what happened to my friend. But sadly, that's not the case with many Christians today. For many Christians, there is nothing different between them and the world. They live like the world, act like the world, and talk like the world. For a genuine believer in Christ, their life must be different from the life of a non-believer. This does not make the Christian better. We are all sinners before God. It just makes the Christian forgiven.

During Jesus' earthly ministry, John wrote:

> John 7:37-38, "On the last and most important day of the festival, Jesus stood up and cried out, 'If anyone is thirsty, he should come to Me and drink! The one who believes in Me, as the Scripture has said, will have streams of living water flow from deep within him.'"

This leads to the second metaphor in Revelation 22:17. The "living water" is a direct reference to the "river of living water."

> Revelation 22:1, "Then he showed me the river of living water, sparkling like crystal, flowing from the throne of God and of the Lamb."

This living water nourishes the Tree of Life and gives the tree its eternal properties. As you and I live in the New Jerusalem and eat from the Tree of Life, we experience eternal life. Believers receive eternal life the moment they accept Jesus as their Savior, but we do not experience eternal life until we arrive in Heaven and start living it.

WHY DOES JESUS WARN US NOT TO TAMPER WITH GOD'S WORD?

Before concluding the book, John gives a personal warning to those (present and future) who deliberately alter the message of the Bible.

What does John mean when he says if anyone adds to God's Word, God will inflict him with plagues (Revelation 15-16), and if anyone takes away from God's Word, God will take away his reward (Revelation 21-22)? Let me state God is not talking about losing one's salvation. The "anyone" John refers to is the false teachers who had gone out to deceive the believers of his day. It was common practice in the Old Testament to warn those who may want to tamper with God's Word:

> Deuteronomy 4:2, "You must not add anything to what I command you or take anything away from it, so that you may keep the commands of the Lord your God I am giving you."

> Deuteronomy 12:32, "You must be careful to do everything I command you; do not add anything to it or take anything away from it."

Tampering with God's Word is a serious matter, and it's a sign of unbelief. Satan is an unbeliever. The false teachers are unbelievers, and everyone that alters God's Word is an unbeliever. This was so serious that John told the "elect lady" in 2 John to not even say, "Welcome" to the false teacher. If she did, she shared in his evil work (v. 11). Don't let them in your house. Don't let them speak to your children. Don't give them the time of day.

SINCE JESUS IS COMING AGAIN, WHY HASN'T HE ALREADY COME?

Jesus' Second Coming is Heaven's greatest secret:

> Matthew 24:36, "Now concerning that day and hour no one knows—neither the angels in heaven, nor the Son—except the Father only."

Many have predicted Jesus' Second Coming, claiming they know the day He will return, but the truth is no one knows when Jesus will return. If God's closest companions in Heaven, Jesus and the angels, don't know, you can bet no person on Earth knows. What should you do with the Second Coming prognosticators? Ignore them! They have been wrong! Jesus' Second Coming is Top Secret information. It's classified. No one knows, but God Himself.

If we knew the day Jesus returns, we would party as if there was no tomorrow, then get saved at the last minute. We lose the urgent expectation of His return.

I find it interesting that Jesus links His Second Coming to Noah's Ark in the Old Testament.

> Matthew 24:37-39, "As the days of Noah were, so the coming of the Son of Man will be. For in those days before the flood they were eating and drinking, marrying and giving in marriage, until the day Noah boarded the ark. They didn't know until the flood came and swept them all away. So this is the way the coming of the Son of Man will be."

Noah's Ark is one of the most maligned events in the Bible. People scoff at the belief of Noah's Ark and a worldwide flood. But it's not the only Old Testament event linked to Jesus. Jonah and the whale are also linked to Jesus' burial and resurrection. Notice what Jesus said:

> Matthew 12:40-41, "For as Jonah was in the belly of the huge fish three days and three nights, so the Son of Man will be in the heart of the earth three days and three nights. The men of Nineveh will stand up at the judgment with this generation and condemn it, because they repented at Jonah's proclamation; and look—something greater than Jonah is here!"

God links two of the most mocked events in the Old Testament with two of the most important events in the Bible—the Resurrection and the Second Coming. Jesus said He would rise from the dead, and He did. He said that He is coming again, and He will.

The Second Coming is a fact! No one in the Christian community argues this. We may debate how Jesus is coming, but we do not debate that

He is coming. In Revelation 22:20, John echoes Jesus' other two announcements that He is coming quickly (vv. 7, 12).

When I go to churches to speak on the Second Coming, I begin the presentation by asking, "Are you ready for Jesus to return?" The majority answers with an enthusiastic, "YES!"

I can honestly say I am ready. I'm tired of dealing with temptation and sin. If it were up to me, I would tell Jesus to come back today. Let's get life over with and move on to eternity.

Since Jesus is coming, why hasn't He already come? Why has He delayed? I believe the apostle Peter gives us two reasons:

> 2 Peter 3:8-9, "Dear friends, don't let this one thing escape you: with the Lord one day is like 1,000 years, and 1,000 years like one day. The Lord does not delay His promise, as some understand delay, but is patient with you, not wanting any to perish, but all to come to repentance."

1. God is on a timetable that frees Him from human restrictions (v. 8). If we take this verse literally, then Jesus' Ascension 2,000 years ago has just been two days. The point Peter makes is that God is not bound by time restrictions on Earth. He has an eternal timetable that we cannot comprehend, nor should we try. We should trust God that He is omnipotent, omniscient, and omnipresent. He knows best.

2. God is patient, wanting everyone to repent (v. 9). Romans 11:25 says, "A partial hardening has come to Israel until the full number of the Gentiles has come in." What does this mean? It doesn't mean a scoreboard is in Heaven and as soon as God saves the last Gentile, Jesus will come back. It means, right now, God is giving the Gentiles an opportunity to accept His salvation. When Peter says that God delays, it's important to understand, God's delay is not what we think. When we think of delay, we think of something that should have happened, but was hindered. When God delays, it's because He determines it's not time for it to happen. This doesn't mean it won't happen, it simply means it's not time.

Why has God delayed Jesus' return? I believe according to 2 Peter 3:9, it's because He wants as many people to be saved as possible. So, what do we do until Jesus' return? Be holy in conduct and in godliness.

> 2 Peter 3:11-12, "Since all these things are to be destroyed in this way, it is clear what sort of people you should be in holy conduct and godliness as you wait for and earnestly desire the coming of the day of God."

John concludes the book of Revelation with a blessing (v. 21). It was meant for the seven churches of Revelation 2-3. But, led by the Spirit, John's last words are a prayer for believers:

> Revelation 22:20-21, "Amen! Come, Lord Jesus! The grace of the Lord Jesus be with all the saints. Amen."

7 Points of Review

1. Heaven is eternal and forever, but it's also the end. The end of death as we know it. The end of sin as we know it. The end of time as we know it.

2. Jesus coming quickly is a reference to the Rapture and the Second Coming. It's both a warning and a reward.

3. The five titles of Jesus mentioned in 22:13 and 16 show Jesus transcends all time and all places.

4. The call to "Come" is from the Holy Spirit and the Bride and for the world to receive Jesus as their Savior.

5. Tampering and altering God's Word is a serious matter. It is a sign of unbelief.

6. The Second Coming is a fact! And when He comes, it will be quick (22:7, 12, 20).

7. The Old Testaments accounts of "Jonah and the Whale" and "Noah's Ark" are two of the most maligned events in the Bible. But God links them to the most important events in the Bible—Jesus' Resurrection and His Second Coming.

1. Daniel is told to seal the prophetic words of his book, while John is told to keep the prophetic words of his book open. What has changed between Daniel's prophecy and John's revelation?

   _____

   _____

   _____

   _____

2. When Jesus comes, it's a warning (v. 11). What's the warning? When Jesus comes, it's a reward (v. 12). What's the reward?

   _____

   _____

   _____

   _____

3. Looking back in the Introduction, what are the four visions of John in Revelation?

   _____

   _____

   _____

   _____

4. Why is tampering with God's Word a serious matter?

_____

_____

_____

_____

5. Why hasn't Jesus already come?

_____

_____

_____

_____

MOTIVATION:

- What's the best reward you have ever received? What is the best reward you've given someone?

- If you knew you were dying, what would be your last words? Who would you tell them to?

EXAMINATION:

- Jesus gives five titles for Himself in Revelation 22:12-16. What do these five titles teach you about Jesus?

- Discuss the two reasons given for why Jesus hasn't returned. Brainstorm more reasons.

APPLICATION:

- Make a list of the things or people you admire. Have you elevated them above God? Anything or anyone you answer "Yes!" about needs to be removed from your life, or lowered to a proper place.

- The last two verses of the Bible are a prayer. Write this prayer on a card and pray for the rapid return of Jesus.

FINAL THOUGHT

CHAPTER THIRTEEN: SINCE HEAVEN IS REAL, SO IS HELL

People often view Hell as the other place you go to when you die. It's not that bad. It's a perpetual party with your friends. We tell jokes about Hell. We laugh about Hell. People even talk about going to Hell. But Hell is no joke. It's not the other place you go to when you die, it's the place where God doesn't exist. Many people do not believe in Heaven, but more people do not believe in Hell.

Jesus believed in Hell. Revelation says, He holds the keys to the Abyss (Revelation 1:18). He chains up Satan, the Dragon, and throws him into the Abyss, closing and sealing it for 1,000 years (Revelation 20:1-3). Jesus had many encounters with Satan and his demons in the Bible (Matthew 4:1-11; 17:14-23; Mark 1:21-28; 3:20-30; 5:1-17; 16:9, 17; Luke 9:1; 22:31). Those encounters prove Satan and his demons are real. The Bible gives us some concrete facts about Hell:

- God created Hell for Satan and the fallen angels (Matthew 25:41).

- Hell is grief (Matthew 8:12).

- Hell is eternal death (Revelation 2:11).

- Hell is destruction (2 Thessalonians 1:9).

- Hell is torment (Luke 16:23).

- Hell is complete darkness (Matthew 22:13; 25:30).

- Hell is a bottomless pit (Revelation 20:3).

- Hell is the Lake of Fire (Revelation 20:14).

- Hell is weeping, wailing, and gnashing of teeth (Matthew 25:30).

- Hell is permanent separation from God (Revelation 20:11-15).

There are two questions everyone asks regarding God and Hell:

1. How is Hell a fair punishment for sin?

2. How can a loving God send people to Hell?

HOW IS HELL A FAIR PUNISHMENT FOR SIN?

Many people dislike thinking about Hell because they believe it's unfair. This comes from a misunderstanding of who God is, who man is, and what sin is. To understand why Hell is a fair punishment for sin, one needs to understand the nature of God, the nature of man, and the nature of sin.

The Nature of God: God is kind, loving, merciful, holy, and righteous. But God also hates sin and will not tolerate it.

> Proverbs 6:16-19, "The Lord hates six things; in fact, seven are detestable to Him: arrogant eyes, a lying tongue, hands that shed innocent blood, a heart that plots wicked schemes, feet eager to run to evil, a lying witness who gives false testimony, and one who stirs up trouble among brothers."

God hates what sin has done to His creation. When He created the world, it was perfect. Satan and sin have destroyed what was perfect. So, put yourself in God's place. You created something, which you are very proud of, but someone comes along and destroys everything you have created. How angry would you be? Maybe now you understand how God feels. His nature is to love. No true believer argues this. But it's also true God hates sin.

The Nature of Man: Humanity is hopelessly sinful. We have been that way since Adam and Eve. Because God is perfect, all sin contradicts God's nature. David committed adultery with Bathsheba, and had her husband, Uriah, murdered. The Prophet Nathan confronted David. Notice what David prayed:

> Psalm 51:1-5, "Be gracious to me, God, according to Your faithful love; according to Your abundant compassion, blot out my rebellion. Wash away my guilt, and cleanse me from my sin. For I am conscious of my rebellion, and my sin is always before me. Against You—You alone—I have sinned and done this evil in Your sight. So You are right when You pass sentence; You are blameless when You judge. Indeed, I was guilty when I was born; I was sinful when my mother conceived me."

David knew he had sinned against Bathsheba and Uriah, but first, he had sinned against God. The same goes for you and me. We sin against ourselves and others, but every sin we commit is against God. Hell is a fair punishment because God is perfect and humanity is sinful.

The Nature of Sin: Since all sin is against God, all sins must be punished. Since sin is constant on the Earth and God is omnipotent, omniscient, and omnipresent, our sin is always before Him. He must punish our sin to satisfy His eternal and perfect nature.

A person in Hell understands God's nature, his own nature, and sin's nature better than anyone on Earth. The rich man and Lazarus are a perfect illustration (Luke 16:19-31). The rich man, and every inhabitant in Hell, knows they deserve to be there. They know they are in Hell by their own choosing. Their greatest torment is knowing they could have avoided it. They will say to themselves for eternity, "Why didn't I just believe?"

Hell is a fair punishment for sin because Hell is never a punishment for just one sin. Hell is a punishment for a lifetime of sin. Every human being sins every day, multiple times a day. If you live to be eighty years old, you will live 29,220 days. Let's say you commit ten sins per day (and I'm being generous). That adds up to 292,200 sins in a lifetime. If someone sinned against you, when would you say, "Enough"? It would be long before the 292,200th time. Eternity in Hell results from hundreds of thousands of sins.

If you commit a crime against me, there's a good chance the judge will give you probation, or a fine, or limited jail time, depending on the severity of the crime. But if you commit a crime against the President of the United States, it's likely your sentence will be life in prison, regardless of the crime. Why? Because the President is a world leader. God is greater than you, me, and the President. He is God over the entire universe. Our lifetime of sin is greater because it's against the Creator of the Universe.

Hell is a fair punishment for sin because an unbeliever separates himself from God on Earth, and so he separates himself from God in eternity. An unbeliever who rejects Jesus' gift of salvation and lives a life of unforgiven sin understands God will not stand in the way of their choice, even though He knows there's an eternal consequence.

HOW CAN A LOVING GOD SEND PEOPLE TO HELL?

When people ask me this question, I always answer: "He doesn't! He desires for all people to be saved" (1 Timothy 2:4). God doesn't send anyone to Hell, each person determines where they will spend eternity. John clearly states who will go to Heaven and who will go to Hell.

> John 3:18, "Anyone who believes in Him is not condemned, but anyone who does not believe is already condemned, because he has not believed in the name of the One and Only Son of God."

In this context, to "believe" doesn't mean to just have knowledge, it also means to have loyalty and allegiance through salvation in Jesus. Those who go to Hell choose not to believe in Jesus.

Hell is everyone's default destination. To go to Hell, you don't have to do a thing. But to go to Heaven, you must accept Jesus as your Savior. If you don't, Hell is your eternal destination.

God doesn't send anyone to Hell. He honors one's choice to go there. God takes no one to Heaven who holds on to their sin on Earth. The apostle John lays out the problem and solution concerning humanity, Heaven, and Hell:

> John 1:10-13, "He was in the world, and the world was created through Him, yet the world did not recognize Him. He came to His own, and His own people did not receive Him. But to all who did receive Him, He gave them the right to be children of God, to those who believe in His name, who were born, not of blood, or of the will of the flesh, or of the will of man, but of God."

"How can a loving God send people to Hell?" is the wrong question. The correct question is: "How can anyone reject a loving God, and choose to go to Hell?" The Apostle Paul gives us the reason:

> Romans 1:18-20, "For God's wrath is revealed from heaven against all godlessness and unrighteousness of people who by their unrighteousness suppress the truth, since what can be known about God is evident among them, because God has shown it to them. For His invisible attributes, that is, His eternal power and divine nature, have been clearly seen since the creation of the world, being understood through what He has made. As a result, people are without excuse."

People "suppress the truth" on purpose. It's "evident among them" and "clearly seen" and "being understood through what He has made," they have turned away and refuse to see God's truth. God has made His attributes visible for everyone to see. Those who choose not to believe it, "are without excuse."

WHICH ROAD ARE YOU ON?

The punishment of Hell is about the torment. But it's also about the agony of knowing God removes you from His presence. Those in Hell know why they are there, and they could have easily avoided it.

Many believe Satan is the ruler of Hell. He might be. But Satan and his demons are part of the tormented in Hell. Since God rules over the universe, He also rules over Hell. Just as the Bible teaches that Satan is the ruler of the world, it also teaches that God is the ruler over the universe, which includes Hell.

> Luke 12:4-5, "And I say to you, My friends, don't fear those who kill the body, and after that can do nothing more. But I will show you the One to fear: Fear Him who has authority to throw people into hell after death. Yes, I say to you, this is the One to fear!"

God has the power to throw you into Hell because He holds the keys to death and Hades.

> Revelation 1:18, "I was dead, but look—I am alive forever and ever, and I hold the keys of death and Hades."

These two passages show the Ruler of the universe is the Ruler of Hell. God created Hell for the Devil and his demons (Matthew 25:41), and states most people will end up in Hell:

> Matthew 7:13-14, "Enter through the narrow gate. For the gate is wide and the road is broad that leads to destruction, and there are many who go through it. How narrow is the gate and difficult the road that leads to life, and few find it."

The many on the "wide" road have one thing in common: they rejected Jesus. The few on the "narrow" road have one thing in common: they accepted Jesus.

The night before my father died, we were in the emergency room at the hospital in DeFuniak Springs, Florida. I was sitting in the waiting room when a nurse asked me to go to dad's room to consult with the doctor. Dad needed a test on his heart, but he was refusing. The doctor said to dad, "Mr. Oliver, if we don't run this test, you could die." Dad looked at the doctor, then at me, and said, "Whether I live or die is between Jesus and me."

There were times when I wasn't sure which road my father was on, but the night before he died, he let me know he was on the narrow road that leads to Jesus.

So, which road are you on? When Jesus said He's the only way to Heaven (John 14:6), that's what He meant. If you are following anyone other than Him, you are on the wrong road.

7 Points of Review

1. The world has taken the sting out of Hell by telling jokes about it. By making it the other place you go to when you die, Hell has become a party place with your friends. But, Hell is no joke. There will be no party in Hell. It's total darkness and complete loneliness. It's the worst place imaginable. The suffering is eternal.

2. Jesus had many encounters with Satan and his demons. God recorded them in the Bible. Those encounters show Satan and his demons are real.

3. Many people dislike the idea of Hell because they believe it's not fair. This comes from a misunderstanding about the nature of God, the nature of man, and the nature of sin.

4. David knew his sin was against God. The same goes for you and me. You may sin against yourself or others, but ultimately, your sin is against God.

5. As illustrated in the chapter, eternity in Hell is not about a few sins. Eternity in Hell results from hundreds of thousands of sins over a lifetime.

6. Many people ask, "How can a loving God send people to Hell?" This is the wrong question. The right question: "How can anyone reject a loving God, and choose to go to Hell?"

7. An unbeliever who separates himself from God on Earth separates himself from God in eternity. God will not stand in the way of their choice.

1. What are the facts about Hell mentioned in the chapter?

   _____

   _____

   _____

   _____

2. Why is Hell a fair punishment for a lifetime of sin?

   _____

   _____

   _____

   _____

3. How do you describe the nature of God, the nature of man, and the nature of sin?

   _____

   _____

   _____

   _____

4. After reading the chapter, how do you answer a person who asks, "How can a loving God send people to Hell?"

_____

_____

_____

_____

5. According to Luke 12:4-5 and Revelation 1:8, why should an unbeliever fear God?

_____

_____

_____

_____

Group Discussion Guide

MOTIVATION:

- Do you know any jokes about Hell? Share, if they are G-rated.

- Discuss the seriousness of Hell, and why the world labels it the other place people go when they die.

EXAMINATION:

- Using Matthew 4:1-11, Jesus' temptations in the wilderness, make a list of the things you discovered about Satan in his encounter with Jesus.

- Using John 1:10-13, discuss the problem and solution concerning humanity, Heaven, and Hell.

APPLICATION:

- Are you on the wide road that leads to Hell, or the narrow road that leads to Heaven?

- Pray for at least one person you know, who is on the wide road.

BIBLIOGRAPHY

Alcorn, Randy. Heaven: A Comprehensive Guide to Everything the Bible Says About Our Eternal Home. Carol Stream, Ill: Tyndale, 2004.

Anders, Max. Holman New Testament Commentary. Nashville, TN: Broadman & Holman Publishers, 2000.

Eareckson-Tada, Joni. Heaven: Your Real Home. Grand Rapids, MI: Zondervan, 1995.

Hanegraaff, Hank. Resurrection. Nashville, TN: Thomas Nelson, 2000

Jeffress, Robert, Dr. A Place Called Heaven. Grand Rapids, MI: Baker Books, 2017.

MacArthur, John. The MacArthur New Testament Commentary. Chicago, Ill: Moody Publishers, 2008.

McGee, J. Vernon, Thru The Bible. Nashville, TN: Thomas Nelson Publishers, 1983.

Oliver, Neale, Dr. All About The Second Coming Of Christ. Bloomington, IN: Westbow Press, 2019.

Panagore, Peter Baldwin. Heaven Is Beautiful. New York: Guidepost, 2015.

Pentecost, J. Dwight. Things To Come. Grand Rapids, MI: 1958.

Scott, Walter. Exposition of the Revelation of Jesus Christ. London: Pickering and Inglis, n.d.

Weirsbe, Warren. The Bible Exposition Commentary. Colorado Springs, CO: Chariot Victory Publishing, 1989.

ABC'S OF SALVATION

God never intended salvation to be difficult. His plan of salvation is simple enough for you to understand. In fact, it's as easy as ABC.

ADMIT

Admit that you are a sinner. The Bible says that everyone has a problem with sin, from the richest to the poorest, from the youngest to the oldest.

> Romans 3:23, "For all have sinned, and fall short of the glory of God."

> Romans 6:23, "For the wages of sin is death, but the gift of God is eternal life through Christ Jesus our Lord."

BELIEVE

Believe that Jesus Christ is the Son of God and that He died on the cross to forgive you of all your sins. He is the only way to salvation and the only way to eternity in Heaven. You have done nothing to deserve God's salvation; He gives it to you because He loves you.

> John 3:16, "For God so loved the world in this way: He gave his One and Only Son, so that everyone who believes in Him will not perish, but have eternal life."

> John 14:6, "Jesus told him, "I am the way and the truth and the life. No one comes to the Father except through me."

CONFESS

Confess your sins and commit your life to Jesus Christ.

> 1 John 1:9, "If we confess our sins, he is faithful and righteous to forgive us our sins and to cleanse us from all unrighteousness."

> Romans 10:9-10, "If you confess with your mouth, 'Jesus is Lord,' and believe in your heart that God raised Him from the dead, you will be saved. One believes with the heart, resulting in righteousness, and one confesses with the mouth, resulting in salvation."

PRAY

Lord Jesus, I know I'm a sinner. But I believe You died on the cross to forgive me of my sins. I believe You were raised from the dead on the third day, and now You are in Heaven preparing an eternal home for me. I accept you as my Savior, my Lord, and my Friend. Thank you for giving me the gift of eternal life. I love you.

ENDNOTES

Robert Jeffress, *A Place Called Heaven*, (Baker Books, Grand Rapids, MI., 2017), 100.

Greg Laurie, Croowalk.com, "Death Is Not The End" (Greg Laurie Daily Devotion), December 26, 2017.

Billy Graham, billygrahamlibrary.org/blog-10-quotes-from-billy-graham-on-heaven.

Randy Alcorn, *Heaven*, (Tyndale, Carol Stream, Ill., 2004), 59.

J. Vernon McGee, *Thru The Bible Commentary, Vol. 5*, (Thomas Nelson Publishers, Nashville, TN., 1983), 75.

Randy Alcorn, *Heaven: A Comprehensive Guide to Everything the Bible Says About Our Eternal Home*, (Tyndale, Carol Stream, Ill.,2004), quote, R.A. Torrey, 112.

Neale B. Oliver, *All About The Second Coming of Christ*, (Westbow Press, Bloomington, IN., 2019), 25-40.

Stories for the Heart compiled by Alice Gray (Multnomah, Portland, OR., 1996), 15.

all-greatquotes.com/if-you-could-see-where-i-have-gone-sympathy-poems-funeral-poems/

Sermonillustrations.com/a-z/a/angels

Peter Baldwin Panagore, *Heaven Is Beautiful*, (Guideposts, New York, 2015), 182.

J. Vernon McGee, *Thru The Bible Commentary, Vol. 5*, (Thomas Nelson Publishers, Nashville, TN., 1983), 1069

sermonillustrations.com/a-z/h/heaven.

Wikipedia, The Free Encyclopedia, Christ Cathedral (Garden Grove, California).

Randy Alcorn, *Heaven*, (Tyndale, Carol Stream, Ill.,2004), quote, R.A. Torrey, 258.

Randy Alcorn, *Heaven*, (Tyndale, Carol Stream, Ill.,2004), quote, R.A. Torrey, 428.

MORE FROM
DR. NEALE B. OLIVER

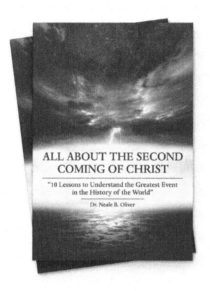

All About The Second Coming of Christ

The Second Coming of Christ is fact. And it is a culmination of thousands of years of Bible prophecy. Jesus' return will reveal the future of the Jews, Gentiles, and the Christian church. His return will also reveal the eternity of both the saved and unsaved. All About The Second Coming of Christ by Dr. Neale B. Oliver is expertly devoted to this truth, and it comes from over 20 years of research, study, and teaching about the greatest event in the history of the world. In this book, Pastor Neale takes you on a journey to understand what the Bible teaches about the events surrounding Jesus' return.

Not a seminary textbook, each chapter of All About The Second Coming of Christ is tailored for the average person sitting in the church pew—one who desires to know what the Bible teaches about the Second Coming. When you finish reading this book, you will have a greater understanding of the events of Christ's return as they unfold through the pages of the Bible.

In the end analysis, All About The Second Coming of Christ was written to alert the world that Jesus is coming again—and it could happen today!

Where Heaven might be, what it might look like, whether your spouse will still be your spouse there, how you will fill your time, and a million other questions? And most of all, will you get to talk with God?

Grab your copy today at (link)

MONDAY MINUTE

WITH PASTOR NEALE

Each Monday Pastor Neale posts a short video on his Facebook page. Each video offers a synopsis of his Sunday's message, a related topic to the message, or one simple point from the message.

www.facebook.com/noliverbooks

MORE FROM PASTOR NEALE

Website: noliverbooks.com

Facebook: www.facebook.com/noliverbooks